Erika Burton, BSW

The Unrelenting Call
of the
Unseen Child

Holistic Trauma Healing for the Inner Child

To Every Survivor of Childhood Abuse—

It was not your fault, you are so beautiful and you are not alone.

Table of Contents

Introduction..1

Chapter 1: I Can Tell You...2

Chapter 2: All My Fault..15

Chapter 3: My Own Prison..35

Chapter 4: This Little Flicker of Light....................46

Chapter 5: The Psycho Mother.................................60

Chapter 6: Alone in the Swirling Abyss...................71

Chapter 7: Out of Control...90

Chapter 8: My Choice...104

Chapter 9: Terrified..118

Chapter 10: The Call of that Little Girl.................135

Chapter 11: Stifling My Voice................................148

Chapter 12: Like Sharks Who've Smelled Blood..........166

Chapter 13: Good Girl..182

Chapter 14: True Power Within.............................195

About the Author..203

Introduction

I wrote this book as a piecing together of my healing journey. It wasn't linear and I didn't remember it in the sense of start to finish. And so, I wrote this book in a similar fashion to how I went down this path. I am sharing with you some of the intimate details of the childhood sexual and psychological abuse I experienced along with the heart-wrenching pain and debilitating shame I felt as an adult remembering. I wanted to attempt to put into words how I felt as a child and as an adult remembering because I am only one of many others who have been abused and I wanted to try to speak for those who cannot speak for themselves. In bringing out into the light that which they wanted kept in the dark for all the days, it is my heart-felt dream that the cries of the unseen children will be heard. I hope that this book awakens in you that little spark and that you find the courage to listen to the call of the unseen child both within you and without.

Chapter 1:

I Can Tell You...

Sometimes I just want to forget it all happened and pretend that I grew up in one of those families they portray in the movies. You know the ones with the laughter-filled family dinners, the reminiscing over the memories and the good-natured jokes? There was a time when I did play make-believe. I buried it all away deep inside of me. I shoved it all down so that I could pretend that I was okay. I mean, they demanded that I keep it that way. There were things you just don't talk about, stuff you keep just "in the family". And they shamed me for doing it. First, they championed for it and trained me to do it and then they blamed and shamed me for doing it. So, I really didn't want to talk about it. It was so gross and disgusting that they did those things to me and that I did those things; I didn't want anyone to know.

It makes it kind of hard to explain some of these things if you don't understand what it is. If you're not willing to look at the shame and open up those dark corners inside yourself where you've buried those dirty secrets from the past, it's going to make it difficult to see it. I say this because that was once me. I pretended that I was okay. I told myself that these kinds of things only happen to other kids. I lied to myself about the abuse that had happened and chalked all my inner pain up to me being the problem. So, if I have to be the one to burst your fantasy bubble, well then, here I am. The abuse I endured isn't just a one-off experience. I really wish that it was but frankly, if it happened to me, a white girl from a well-off Christian family that no one would have ever considered, then it's been happening everywhere.

I can tell you that I wasn't the only kid being abused sometimes. I can tell you what happened in some of the board rooms at the various churches we attended where the church men went to their men's only Sunday School classes. I can tell you about those rooms where they sat in a circle on plastic office chairs and had us kids naked in the middle. I can tell you how we had to dance for them and show them our bodies. I can tell you how they demanded we come over to them and how they touched us and put their hands all over us. I can tell you about sitting on their knees, straddling them with my "pee-pee" spread open on their legs. I can tell you about riding around up and down while they played with my nipples. I can tell you about the other man standing behind that guy pushing his penis into my mouth and the cum (the "gross stuff") running down my face. I can tell you about dancing around naked in front of these men until I was summoned to one of them.

I can tell you how he made me put one leg up on his shoulder while leaving the other on the floor, completely spread open for him. I felt very nervous. Very open. Very ashamed. Scared. Not knowing what would happen next. And also, very aroused and excited. I wondered what he would do next, waiting anxiously for his touch. Would it hurt? Would it feel good? I wanted it and I didn't want it and I can get "excited" writing about it (which is a whole other can of worms because for so long, I was so ashamed that I was sometimes excited and that I did sometimes have fun. I felt like I must have been such a bad person for wanting it. It was hard to acknowledge that it was never my fault, the child. I was conditioned and trained that way. It would have been heresy or blasphemy to even think that it was the fault of the adults who exposed and trained me in these ways).

I couldn't hold the position very well. It hurt my legs but I tried to hold it. He started touching me and putting his fingers in me and his fist, it was like he was punching me. I started crying and he slapped me. He told me to stop bawling. And his hand that he was punching me inside with was the one he slapped me with. I saw the blood and I couldn't stop the tears. And so, he called over some people or some people just came over and they took me to the room they said was for kids who wanted to cry. And in this dimly lit room, on the white with grey speckles floor, with more of the hard plastic chairs, some stacked and some not, they put me on the floor. They tied me up with all my hands and feet up together while I was on my back. They dumped oil or something slimy like oil all over me and I was filled with shame. I felt so embarrassed because I knew that when I would leave, everyone would know because I would be all covered in this oil, my hair and everything. They slid me all around the floor, like bumper cars, running me into things. And honestly, I was so concerned about what everyone would think of me that I hardly noticed. I was overwhelmed by this feeling that I'd never get the guck off of me. I was in this state of shock I guess, disgust at myself for crying, for doing it wrong, for getting in trouble. I was wondering how I could do it better next time, how I could get it all right and not get in trouble. Why did I always have to cry? And just thinking about it would make me start crying again and so, I would feel ashamed, like it was my fault all over again.

And I can see now how this is exactly where they wanted me to be, stuck in this cycle of blaming myself and holding myself as the only one responsible. I remember standing another time, just like that, but this time I got it right; I held the position and I didn't fall over. I must have practiced it over and over in my mind a hundred times so that I would get it right. So, I was very proud that I had done a good job and gotten it right. And he touched me and it felt so good. He slid his hand over and over me. He put his hand somewhere and kept getting it all oily. He kept going around and around on my pee-pee and my bum with his oily hand. Eventually, he pulled me closer to him and I started to fall. Someone was behind me though and they caught me. They held me there with my legs spread over their arms. They kept my legs apart and held my pee-pee up in front of the man's face. And his face was so happy and red and I got such a big embarrassed feeling inside. I stood there, watching him, as he made my pee-pee feel so funny and good. He told me what a good girl I was and that I looked so yummy and wet. He reached his hand up and with his thumb, he stroked over my pee-pee and as much as I felt like a good girl, I also felt like a really bad girl.

Then he put something inside me and I couldn't stop myself from squirming around. There was a sound like I was peeing and I felt so embarrassed again, or still (I'm not sure I ever stopped feeling that way the whole time). He growled and either he or the person holding me, put my pee-pee to his mouth and he started growling all over it. It was so much. It was so great. And it hurt and I couldn't do anything. I tried to shut my legs but the person holding me stopped me. I tried to grab at his head with my hands and I couldn't because the person holding me had somehow pinned my hands down too. It was so much and it hurt and it felt good. So, I screamed uncontrollably. I started crying and freaking out because I couldn't get away.

And there was nothing I could do. Over and over again, there was nothing I could do. Eventually, I just shut down. I closed off the part of myself that cared. I stopped fighting. I quit trying to get away. I shut-down feeling as much as I could, both physically and emotionally. I'm not sure whether it was consciously or if my body just unconsciously did it to protect me or a combination of the two. I would lie to myself about what was happening and how I felt about it occurring. I just sort of went through the motions, somewhat like a robot, I guess. And eventually, I started to just exist in this floating state, this state where I was far-away, where I lied to myself about caring. I would pretend that I was fine and I would just keep making these goals to work towards. I would focus on something tangible that I could achieve that would make me feel better. Better grades, more words written, more crafts done, more volunteering, eating less food, exercising for two hours instead of one hour, only some frozen veggies for my food for the day, ten books read in a week, never getting anything wrong/never making a mistake (here, a part of me was always certain I could achieve this and of course, I always failed, and so the punishments were accepted—the ones I gave myself and the ones I accepted, welcomed even, from others).

For a long time, I hated writing about this. I would feel like throwing up and crying and exploding. I would get so excited and ashamed and I hated that they all thought this was okay. I would hate that I was stuck inside writing this instead of doing something else, being with my kids or anything else. I felt like I would even rather be cleaning and I don't really even like cleaning. I thought then that that would make me feel better, at least for a little bit, because then I could at least pretend that this wasn't all real. But I also hated that me giving in to that feeling let them get away with it, with no one knowing the truth of what they did, because there I was, years later and they still were walking around scotch-free. And I wondered if there was even a point in writing about this, if anyone will even care or if anyone will actually do anything about it. It makes me sick that so many people are hurting kids, each and every day, and people are so stuck up in their fancy houses or the latest show that they don't seem to give two flying donkeys about what is happening to the kid next door. It angers me that people would rather hold grudges over who got the best Christmas present last year while some kids are cringing that it's Christmas again because they don't want to play any more "special" Santa games or be another "special" present.

I can tell you how it felt to have everyone blame me for what they were doing to me. When I couldn't keep all the emotional pain inside and it bled out into an eating disorder (anorexia), anxiety, panic attacks and nightmares, self-harm and low self-esteem, my family blamed me for choosing to "act out" this way. They said that I was the one making myself sick with an eating disorder. I just was too emotional and couldn't handle all the moves we had had. That was their excuse. My mother questioned how smart I really was if I was doing this to myself. On and on they would go with little digs and I would believe them. When I was a young adult my mother went so far as to state that I had a cruel heart because I dared to express to her some of the hurt and pain I had inside from some of the things she had done. She literally ran away crying that I had hurt her by bringing up some of the things she had done (or not done) and then got my dad by her side. Together they tag-teamed me, telling me I needed to leave because I was causing them too much pain.

But when I really look at it, they were done with me because I wouldn't bow down anymore and do things their way. I mean, it's not like it is said straight up like that. But it's a cult and there are rules to follow. And if you don't follow them, well, they punish you in a myriad of ways to get you to comply and fall back in line. If you don't—well then, you are cut off, banished, removed, ostracized and labelled the "black sheep". Some will even go so far as to pretend you never even existed. To them, they'd rather just have no daughter than to have me be the real me. They wanted an obedient dog who came when they called, sat when commanded and offered up myself and my children whenever they demanded.

And when I said no, they left and said there wasn't any hope of reconciliation. To them, reconciliation meant me bowing down and saying I was wrong and they were right. It meant me hiding myself and squeezing into the little box they labelled acceptable for me. It meant pretending they hadn't and weren't abusing me. It meant being a quiet, compliant little (big) girl who fit the image they wanted. And if I would have been willing to admit guilt, say I was wrong and beg for forgiveness, as well as accept whatever punishment they would have demanded and provided the payment for their "graciousness", then they totally would have "forgiven and forgotten". They would have "put the past in the past", so to speak.

I can tell you about the circles in the church gymnasiums. I remember standing there in the center of the circle. I would stand there with a circle of men and boys around me. I would take my clothes off...sometimes I would just be there in the center of the circle. They would all stand there and look at me. And honestly, this was a memory I revisited a lot as a child. I liked it, I guess. It was highly erotic for me, I suppose. Compared to the other things that happened to me, this was something that was pretty mild. It was something I was groomed to do so it felt normal to me. Sometimes they would touch me, sometimes I would touch myself. Sometimes I would just drip all over the floor. Sometimes they would be naked, sometimes they would not. I guess it happened frequently enough that the memories kind of blend together. I wasn't always alone either. There were sometimes other circles going on in that gymnasium. It would be busy and they would kind of block off their circles, almost like their own secret show in their special circle. And we just went into the circles, stood in our spots and did as we were told whenever it was our turn. There wasn't really a lot of thought to it. I didn't ask questions or wonder whether I should or shouldn't be doing this. I just did it. It was just how it was.

I can tell you about the back room deals and the sacrificing of children on alters in white dresses. I remember lying on that cold stone table, in this stone, gray-colored, cold, cave-like place. I remember lying on the table in this white dress with no undies or pantyhose on. And I was cold. I was on the table and I was lying there, helpless. They started singing or chanting. They had their hands under my dress and they lifted it up. They poked and they prodded. They had cold hands and they had sharp things. And they held me down or I just couldn't move, I don't know. Sometimes I couldn't move because I was tied down. Sometimes I couldn't move because I was drugged. Sometimes I couldn't move because I was afraid. Sometimes I couldn't move because doing so would get me in trouble and the punishment was worse than this.

Frankly, I knew that this was going to happen anyhow so better just to get it over with without the punishment too. And sometimes I couldn't move because I was just so well-trained and conditioned to do it right that I wouldn't even think of disobeying. Anyhow, this one person had sharp, shiny objects. They were like knives and he looked like he was cutting me, cutting my pee pee-and it hurt. I screamed and I cried. I wanted my mommy but she didn't come and help me. For all I know, she was there watching, helping and holding me down too. All the while, they just kept singing and chanting. It was so horrible, so sadistic and twisted. I was so cold lying on that stone table that hurt my back and I don't know, I guess I fell asleep.

I stopped writing about this all many times through because I felt ashamed. I felt ashamed looking at all the abuse that has been done to me. I would feel triggered remembering and so remembering brought in panic as I started to feel trapped once again. I felt like writing wasn't freeing me, if anything, I felt even more unsafe at first. As much as I wanted to unburden myself from carrying all of the pain, I felt like I was putting a target on my back, which honestly, I didn't really care about…. I cared more about the targets that might be put on my children's backs. I started remembering about the ways I'd tried to talk before…the times I had asked for help and the ways I'd paid for talking. I started to become more afraid. I felt even more helpless. I remembered those who seemed to be (looking back, I wouldn't put it past my parents/the people abusing me to have had some of these be just dressed-up actors or perhaps it was "adult" dress-up) police officers, firefighters, pastors, teachers, counselors, doctors, friends…who had seemed like good choices to confide in and to seek out for help. And it had just turned into a nightmare, over and over again. I'd kept trying but it just got darker and darker. Eventually, I'd slipped into the darkest place I'd been in and I didn't want to go back there. How could I go back there? My kids needed me. I couldn't lose it now. I would also feel like I was being attacked…like they were attacking me. I guess I just went chicken or better, was a good girl and shut my mouth for a long while. I started to feel like what was the use anyway? Anyone who'd ever believed me before had been in on it too so it had not helped—it had just made it worse.

Do you know what it's like to feel completely and utterly alone? Do you know what it is like to feel like there is no one who will save you? I begged God to help me. I cried out over and over asking Him why He was letting this happen to me. Why wouldn't He just make it stop? The church always had answers—pray more, read the Bible more, stop holding on to the past...on and on. It was always my fault. But I eventually reached a point of understanding; it didn't matter how much I tried to stop them even by being a good, little girl. The harsh truth was that if they wanted to, they did it. And I finally realized as an adult that my silence doesn't keep us safe. My silence guarantees nothing except that this sick, perverted, Satanic abuse continues on. So, I've been writing even though that little traumatized girl inside sometimes screams and sobs, begging me to stop. But over time, I really started to listen to her as it started to be less triggering hearing her scream and sob. And I began to wonder if it was actually just a replaying in my mind of the soundtrack of her pleading with them to stop?

Chapter 2

All My Fault

It didn't matter what I said or what I did, it always ended up being my fault. And that has been one of the hardest core programs for me to shake—the belief that it was all my fault. I could sometimes hear the playback in my mind of me screaming and sobbing, "I'm so sorry, I'm so sorry, I'm so sorry" as they raped me, hurt me, threatened and abused me. Sometimes, I could barely remember what had really happened afterwards. It was so brutal, so traumatic, so ungodly and so terrifying. It seemed pointless to remember anyhow because they always knew the true truth, right? There was all of them and only one of me, so they had to be telling the true story (or at least that's what they said).

When I got away from them, my family, that soundtrack started playing back again...when I couldn't get my toddler to stop having tantrums, when I couldn't prevent my husband from getting mad at me, when I couldn't be perfect enough to get it all right, when I couldn't meet the impossible expectations others and I placed on myself. And sometimes the lines blurred between present pain and the tendrils of past, unhealed traumas that resurfaced as I reached higher places of healing. The nuances can be so subtle. And I began to recognize that it's up to me to decide if I want the past to dictate my present. It's up to me to decide if I want to be laying on the floor sobbing as a child because I disappointed someone or if I want to realize that I can be accountable for my actions as well as be present for another's pain. Taking back my power means that I get to decide whether I just bend over and accept the abuse or whether I choose to set up firm, healthy boundaries. Rising up means I no longer believe the lie that I don't deserve to breathe anymore because I didn't get it all right. Healing for me has been about learning grace for others and most importantly, for myself. I've finally come to a place where I realize that as long as I'm hating me, it is very difficult, if not impossible, to heal from this pain and break free from these prison chains I shackled myself in.

No one taught me anything about this stuff. There were no talks about my body parts. There were no teachings about saying no; I was always taught to do exactly what I was told. I knew nothing about setting boundaries or making choices for myself. I wasn't allowed to touch my private parts nor did I really know anything about them. I was shown that I was only good if I was performing, if I was doing it all right. I was left with these constant feelings of inadequacy; I believed that something must be wrong with me because they kept hurting me. So, I kept setting higher and higher expectations for myself. I was constantly moving the bar higher and higher because at least then it was my fault that they were hurting me. If only I had gotten 105% (even if there weren't bonus questions, I somehow convinced myself that I could have done something more to earn extra points).

I had two vaginal surgeries as a child. The first was when I was 6 and the second was when I was 9. The surgeries, I was told, were to remove some excess skin that was growing over my vagina. The pee would get stuck in there and then I would "dribble" on my panties making me wet. When I was 12, I had the same issue and so it was brought up with our new pediatrician. To my surprise, she didn't advocate for surgery like the other one did. She instead told us that most girls who have this issue have it resolved during puberty as their body's natural hormones cause the skin to recede. For the few that that doesn't happen for, the first course of action would be a hormonal cream on the area and that usually takes care of it. Very rarely is surgery ever needed. She proceeded to give me some practical solutions to decrease the dribbling as well as suggested pads if that didn't work. Her peeing technique worked just fine though and I no longer had any wet undies.

I will forever be grateful to that pediatrician who saved me from being forced into a medical procedure against my will that I didn't even need. It begs the question though, why I did have the surgery the other two times? Why would a doctor encourage or endorse such a procedure that was completely unnecessary for the child as my previous pediatrician had done? Why would parents be bothered by waiting 6-8 years to find out if the child's body would naturally resolve this potential problem on its own? If there was no quality of life being affected for the child, wouldn't the parents be supportive and advocating for that? Waiting to see if the child's body naturally resolves the issue seems to be a much more logical and economical (even with health insurance, I can't imagine the costs of not one but two surgeries) option never mind more in the best interests of the child's emotional and mental well-being to not have their body violated in that way for no reason. For that is how I felt about the surgeries…violated, ashamed, embarrassed, upset, alone and afraid.

Over the years, I've had to disclose the surgeries in different scenarios (which was frankly quite embarrassing before that trauma was released) and a lot of medical professionals hadn't even heard of that kind of a surgery. They looked at me kind of strangely. Looking back, maybe they did know of the surgery but were baffled as to why I would have undergone it twice and at such a young age. I later had a medical professional tell me that even years ago before I was a child, surgery wasn't even the first option. She told me that surgery wasn't generally considered unless all other options had failed, the girl was menstruating and there were complications as a result. My parents were medical professionals. Is it really possible that they didn't know about the other less-invasive options? Did they really make me undergo general anesthetic, a terribly embarrassing procedure and a painful recovery because they didn't know?

Or could they have had ulterior motives, you know, ones that weren't in my best interest? It may not have been in their best interests to have to wait until I hit puberty for that piece of skin that was growing over my vaginal opening to recede. I blindly accepted the surgeries because they told me that's what would fix it and that there was no other choice. For all I know, I didn't even have a piece of skin growing over my vagina and they made it all up. So, all these years, I've just accepted what they implicitly told me—that there was something wrong with me because I needed this surgery. I was somehow "broken" because of this problem

I had. I inherently accepted that there must be something wrong with my genitals, a belief which carried on into adulthood and my childbearing years.

Due to this feeling of inadequacy, of my body not being good enough, having problems etc., I was very worried that I would have trouble giving birth to children. This then made me very susceptible to the doctor's medical agenda and interventions during my first pregnancy and child birth. I accepted it when one doctor told me during my first pregnancy that we would just have to wait and see. In other words, she posited that we wouldn't know if pregnancy and childbirth was something I was capable of until I had done it. And even when an OBGYN looked at me in horror when I told her this and reassured me that she always assumes that a woman's body is capable of this natural process, not the other way around, the years of conditioning of me being less than and that there was something wrong with me, pervaded.

I was required to have cream put on my vagina after surgery after the surgery every day. At 9 years of age, my mother didn't let me apply the cream myself. She didn't even suggest it. Granted, I didn't mention it, though probably because I didn't know that I could have been taught or that it was okay for me to touch my privates. She would make me lie on the bed on my back with my pants and panties off while she applied the cream down there on my pee-pee. It hurt. I didn't want her to but she didn't give me a choice. When I cried and complained about it hurting once, she jammed her fingers up into my vagina (well, up there inside me somewhere) and I screamed. She told me to shut up and that it would hurt a lot more if I didn't knock it off. I was kind of in shock, I guess, and afraid. I was scared of my mother and what she could do to me. I watched woodenly as she kneeled on the bed and put her legs over one of my legs. She pushed her hand over my other knee, prying my legs apart. She squirted more of the cream on and then she started rubbing my whole pee-pee.

It hurt and it felt good and it burned and it felt nice. Over and over, I was crying, I was laughing, I was upset, I was happy, I was so confused and I just lied there. It was so much and I was just kind of out of it, in the semi-dissociated state I often went to. I could feel her going inside me and I just kept staring off at the wall. I didn't want to look at her. Then she climbed on top of me, over my face. I couldn't breathe with her jeans and heavy bum over my face. I started screaming, trying to breathe. I tried to push away but she pushed her bum on my face and started moving around. I felt so much inside me, like it was tearing me apart. I kicked and tried to lift my hips up but it didn't do anything. She finally hopped over and I rolled away from her, sobbing. I didn't notice what she was doing but I guess she took her pants and panties off because the next thing I knew, she had grabbed me and I was lying back on the bed the same way. The same thing was happening except now her nakedness was on my face.

Her hairy, wet, slimy, stinky nakedness was on my face and I couldn't breathe again. I slapped at her trying to get away again but she wouldn't stop. She kept going, rubbing herself all over my face. When I slapped at her to stop her, she pulled her hand away from my pee-pee and slapped it as hard as she could it seemed. When I still screamed and cried, she slapped my pee-pee, my sore pee-pee from the surgery, over and over again it seemed while I screamed. I thought she would never stop; it seemed like forever. She lifted her bum off my face enough for me to see her face and told me that I better do a good job and be a good girl or she would do it again. And before I knew it, she was on my face again. She got wetter and wetter all over my face and I couldn't breathe. I tried to get away but I couldn't and it all kind of faded away. I thought maybe I fell asleep. Thinking about it now, I guess I must have passed out.

I was so embarrassed and already humiliated. I felt so alone from all the rest of her maltreatment in regards to the surgeries. It burned like crazy when I peed after having the surgeries as anyone who's had a baby knows. But hey, I guess they don't give out peri-bottles to kids undergoing genital surgery for the sexual benefit of the adults in their lives (oh wait, did I actually write that down?). So, I wouldn't go pee for as long as I could and I was crying there telling her how badly I needed to pee but that I was scared because it would hurt so bad. All she did was yell at me telling me that I was making it way worse than it was. She berated me for making a big deal about nothing and told me to just go pee. I felt so ashamed and alone. So, I just shut down some more inside—the message received that no one really cares how I feel.

Another time when she was putting the cream on me, her face was suddenly down there too and I felt her mouth and tongue on my pee-pee. She looked up at me and told me that mommy will make you feel better before she started again. It was so confusing and I lived in this state of constantly being on edge because I never knew what was going to happen next. A different time when she was applying the cream, she flipped me over onto my stomach and started spanking my bum. I just lay there, pushed in the mattress, wishing this misery would end and steeling myself inside for whatever she was going to do next. Then she climbed on top of me. I could feel her nakedness on my bum and she had both knees on either side of me. She started sliding herself up and down my bum over and over again. She pulled my head up by the hair and kissed my mouth. It hurt when she pulled my hair and my neck ached having her wrench it up like that. I felt her shuddering all over my body. It was just so gross. She finally got off of me and I felt so cold because she'd gotten all her wet all over me, thinking that maybe she had even peed on me. She laughed at me and told me that I was a dirty girl covered in filth. She looked down at herself and then back at me before calling me a dog and demanding that this dog get over there and clean her up.

At this point, I was so gone that I didn't even really do any thinking anymore. I just got up. She put one foot on the bed and kept the other on the floor, her parts spread apart. I didn't move fast enough so she grabbed me by the hair again and shoved my face towards her legs. She demanded that the dog, me, clean her up now. She had her wetness all over her inner thighs and her hairy pee-pee and she made me lick every drop up. It was so disgusting. It smelled like rot and her hairs kept getting in my mouth. I kept gagging but I kept going, with an anxious fervor. She rubbed my head telling me I was a good doggie. She offered me my stuffed bear as a treat. I couldn't stop myself from smiling as I reached for my bear. I always thought I hated the dogs we had growing up because my parents, particularly my dad, gave the dogs way more attention than they gave to me. My remembering has helped me see though that it wasn't actually dogs I hated. I just didn't want to look at the times they treated me worse than any dog they ever owned and the ways they forced me to serve them like

I was a dog while their dogs were treated like children, like royalty even.

When I was in grade 2, I somehow won the school spelling bee. I say "somehow" because I didn't even know there was a spelling bee that day. I was just suddenly in the long line that went all along the outside edge of the cafeteria and I was nervous. But soon, I was at the front of the line. I won the spelling bee with the word "rectangle". I was shocked and happy, nervous too. I also wished I hadn't won. Sometime later, we were off to the next level spelling bee. No one really talked to me about it...we didn't really practice much or at all for it. No one really explained what would happen there. I was just told when it was and that it was a long drive.

It was a sunny day. It was a bright, sunny, spring day when the trees were green and the bushes were full. It was probably close to the end of the school year although I'm not exactly sure. I don't remember everyone who went with us in our beige suburban, just that my mom drove and at least one of my brothers came along. It was a busy room, full of fold-out chairs. I remember having to go to the front of the room and then being told that we had to stand in a line with our backsides facing the people in the crowd (so we couldn't cheat by reading the lips of people in the crowd). I was absolutely mortified that I would have to stand like that. I couldn't focus on the words or anything. I was so nervous, so embarrassed. Everything was kind of grey and hazy for me. It wasn't a very normal reaction for me for these sorts of things. Normally, I was pretty calm and didn't get rattled being up in front of a crowd. But that day I was. I got the first word I was given wrong. I had no idea even what word he was saying or how to spell it...or how to spell anything at all really, I was so freaked out.

I don't remember how long we stayed before we went home. For the longest time, that was all I remembered about the spelling bee. Now I remember the rest or at least more of it. My mom drove us towards home and eventually pulled off somewhere and parked. It was somewhere off in the bush. In that full, green bush on that bright, sunny spring day, she made me get out of the suburban and walk into the bush with her. I could still see the suburban, parked kind of at an angle, blocking the road, now that I think about it. She told me to stand, backside facing her, like at the spelling bee. She started berating me for being embarrassed about standing like that, how could anyone be embarrassed to stand like that, guilting me for them having gone all that way only for me to be so stupid, etc. etc.

Eventually, there I was, lying across her knees with my pants on. She made me take my pants off and then there I was, on her lap lying across it with my bum up, panties only on. I was staring at the ground, just lying limply across her lap. Then she took my panties off; she ripped them or cut them, I don't know which. I just know she wrecked them (or at least I assumed she wrecked them, maybe she just hid them) so I couldn't put them back on later. Then she touched my bum and rubbed her hands all over it while berating me about how I had been such a baby. She took a pen and wrote on my bum cheek. She said that it was the word I got wrong. Maybe she wrote it two times, one time on each cheek, or maybe she wrote it only once. I remember thinking it was in blue pen but maybe that's what I imagined while she was writing it or maybe I saw the blue pen after? I felt so humiliated and ultimately, resigned. In my head I told myself that this was the punishment I deserved because I was so stupid at the spelling bee.

Somewhere along the way, I started to fade away into my safe place. It got hazy and grey around the edges and I started to not really be there anymore. It was just easier that way. I got in less trouble. I didn't cry as much (which coincidentally, got me in less trouble). I asked less questions, both aloud and in my head, which got me in less trouble. But I felt it when she stuck the pen (or something that felt like a pen) in me somewhere--my butt, my vagina, maybe both. It was...embarrassing? And I kind of kicked at her but mostly just lied there with cheeks burning with shame. I focused my thoughts on having gotten the word that I couldn't even remember wrong, fixating on that so that I wouldn't focus on what she was doing. She made me walk back to the suburban with no pants. I could see my brother in the window. I can still see my mother with her squinted eye recording it somehow.

I had to sit naked on my seat on the way home. At one point, she made me go in between the captain's seats on all fours with my face down and bum up pointed toward the windshield. My brother(s) put things in my vagina/bum, I don't know which or maybe both. And I was so embarrassed. I think they were grapes. They were all inside me. I was so scared that I would get sick from them and that they wouldn't come out. I tried to hold very still because I was worried about this very much. I was beyond mortified thinking about having to go to the hospital to have the doctor look at me and take them out. When we got home, she told me to go upstairs and wait for her. I practiced writing out the word I got wrong at my desk while I waited for her. When she came in, she shut the door behind her and locked it. She had some stuff in her hands. She told me/made me lean over the footboard of my bed. She pushed me forward so my feet were dangling off the floor. She tied something around each of my ankles and then tied them to something else. I don't know what it was, I couldn't see. She tied them tight and pulled my legs far apart with them. It was really tight and it hurt but I just lied there and waited. My tummy felt funny and it burned at the back of my eyes. My heart was racing and my mouth was so dry that it was really hard to swallow. She tied a rope to each of my wrists and then tied the ropes to the headboard, one on each side.

I did start to really panic then. It was hard to hold my head up but when I let it down, it was hard to breathe being in the mattress and blanket. No, the quilt. It was on that stupid quilt they got me from the Silver Dollar City, that one they said was so expensive and handmade but that I would like because it was blue. That quilt I hated because what I had wanted them to buy me from there was a lifelike doll that was like a real baby but they wouldn't. They said that was too expensive but this quilt was not, I guess. Anyhow, she showed me this sharp thing and poked me with it. She told me that she was going to get the grapes out with it and I had better hold still or it would hurt. I held still and it hurt anyway.

Then she started hitting me with something on my bum. She was mad at me still, I guess, for getting the word wrong and wasting her time. And I just lied there, trying to breathe. Do I lift my head up or leave it down? Lifting it up makes my neck hurt, laying it down made it hard to breathe. I alternated between the two focusing on that instead of what she was doing. Eventually there she was, getting on the bed. I guess I missed her getting undressed because I was so focused on trying to breathe and the burning pain in my neck. She slid under me, first her head, then her chest was there, her boobs under my face. I licked them as she had taught me to do. It was hard because it hurt my neck and it was even harder to breathe too now with them in my face like that. Her nipples were right there all brown-looking and gross. And then she pulled herself out and turned around.

Her privates were under my face with her knees up and bent. I started to lick the ice cream like she had taught me and I made sure to lick deep in the cone and get it all out. It was gross, it always was. It wasn't good like ice cream at all. And my neck still hurt and it was so hard to breathe. I was getting sweaty from how hard I was trying and I felt so cold at the same time. She squeezed her knees tight around my head and I hated it. I couldn't breathe and her slime was all over my face. And then she let go and I could breathe. I thought she was done but then her legs came around my head, locking me in place and I was stuck against her. I started screaming against her and I couldn't breathe. I tried to move but I was stuck. I felt so scared and I was panicking, terrorized. And then she was loosening her legs and I was just relieved that I could breathe.

She called my brother in and told him to spank me with something while I had to lick the ice cream again. And I was so embarrassed. The tears were burning again at the back of my eyes but I just swallowed them and tried to do my best. The harder I try, the sooner I'll be done was my thought. Finally, they both left and I was alone there. It was a long time; it started to get dark. I guess maybe I fell asleep. Then I heard someone. I thought it was my father because it sounded like him and he didn't really say anything to me. He just went behind me and did something to me. I don't know really. He did something to my bum, my pee-pee, my privates.

He poked and prodded-- I could imagine what his face looked like and I felt so embarrassed. He would always get this look on his face. He would get all pink and when he got like that, I would feel all embarrassed and like I wanted to hide. He pulled my cheeks apart and looked, I guess. And then he was suddenly inside me. I felt certain it was him because he was always so warm and big and it felt a certain way. I didn't see anyone else come into the room but I did fall asleep and I couldn't see behind me so I guess, I can't be sure it was him only. Then he pulled out and his gross-smelling, sticky stuff came out all over my bum, all over the writing. I felt like a dirty animal as he rubbed it all over my bum. I wondered if it erased the spelling word.

Later, they let me out. I don't remember who released me or when it was exactly. I remember it was bright and sunny out so maybe it was the next day or maybe it was still sunny out when they let me out. My mother made me walk around outside in just my shirt and no pants showing my bum with the words on it. The sticky stuff was now dry and crunchy and it hurt a bit in my bum when it kind of pulled apart like glue. Eventually, I went into the barn. Maybe she called me in. She was there with a wheelbarrow full of horse poop. She told me to get in and I guess I didn't do it quick enough or looked disgusted or hesitated because she picked me up and put me in. She put me all in the poop. All I could think about was the poop going all in my pee-pee and that was so bad. I was petrified that I was going to get sick. What if I got another UTI? It seemed like I was always sick and in terrible pain from a UTI and I was so scared of getting another one.

She drove me in the wheelbarrow over to the wall with all the horse leads where they were all tied up fancy-like the way she always did it. I never quite knew why I always felt so weird when I looked over there but now, I know. I've always known. She took me over there and tied one of the leads around my neck. I was lying on my back on the horse poop with my legs draped over each side of the wheelbarrow. After everything else she'd done, I should have been prepared for what she did next but I wasn't. I just watched her, as if from afar again, as she took a pitchfork and put the end of it up inside me. It was like this poking and prodding feeling with this burning sensation. It wasn't as bad though as the terrifying thought resounding in my head about the horse poop being inside me making me sick and sore. I desperately hoped that I wouldn't get another

UTI. They hurt so bad and I always had so many of them. I was panicking that maybe this would make it happen again and I really didn't want that. And I guess I was so absorbed in that thinking that it was a good distraction from what she was doing to me.

Then she made me crawl, like a horse I guess, outside. She pushed me with the pitchfork inside me. She made me go to the corral with the sand or soft rocks, the white ground with the red ring. She sent me around the ring like I was the horse running around and around as she swung the lead and called out at me. She hit me with the lead rope if I was too slow, pulled me to her and petted me when I did a good job, I guess. I keep saying "I guess" because that was the thing, I just never really understood why these things were happening or why they wanted me to do it. It was confusing to me and I was never really sure why. We kept going this way and I was kept in line with the visual reminder of how much worse it could be by the pitchfork leaning up against the corral fence. When I was exhausted, sweaty and not sure I could go on anymore, she made me come over to her. She unzipped her jeans as she was leaning against the red corral fence and all her hair was there. And I licked it like I always did.

It's true. I have felt disgusting writing these things, talking about them, bringing them up. I have wished that they were just some bad nightmare…or even just a fetish like my psychologist once told me. I have felt gross thinking about it, feeling their hands on me again. I felt so gross thinking about her nipples, his penis, her hairy vulva, her fat rolls. I thought about how nasty it just all was. Their spit, their sticky stuff, their stinky stuff. It smelled so bad, all of it. And I wanted to forget the smells and the sounds. I tried to wish away all the things I saw as well as the things I did and the things they did. I wanted to pretend it was all just my imagination or some sick joke even. I felt so gross because I remembered liking it sometimes. There were times that I was turned on thinking and writing about some of it. In the beginning of my healing journey, I then felt even more ashamed, if that was even possible. How could I find it exciting? Maybe they were right and maybe I did want it to happen. Sometimes I wondered if it was my fault that they did these things to me.

Chapter 3

My Own Prison

And they weren't wrong about me liking it sometimes; there were times I wanted it. But what they didn't tell me as a kid and what they don't want you to think about now is that no kid who wasn't abused that way would be wanting it, thinking about it or asking for it. That is only a child who has been groomed and abused. So, whether or not I wanted it, it took a long time to accept that it was not my fault. I would think about how I would never blame some other little girl. Yet, even as much as my brain could see that it was not my fault, for the longest time it was really hard to shake that feeling that it was my fault. And that feeling of it all being my fault spilled over into every area of my life. It was like this stench that was around me and, looking back, I get why people noticed it and used it to their advantage. I don't think it's right but I get why they did it. They've also been forced to do things they don't want.

Just take a look at our society, the sick system that pillages and plunders us, the slaves. Everyone around us is oppressed and people don't want to look at it. They've accepted that there is this hierarchy and then they, consciously and unconsciously, perpetuate this sick cycle from the family system, to the school system, to the work-slave system, to the government system, the justice system, the medical system, and so on. I guess it's part of the reason I was pretty scared of people. I felt like they took advantage of me and I don't like what they did to me. And a part of me has believed that it was my fault that they did those things to me. Sometimes I've felt like I didn't know how to stop them. I mean, I got it, I'm supposed to use my words. Set boundaries. Say no. But they were so much louder, so much more confident and so much more sophisticated it seemed that sometimes I didn't even realize that they got me to agree. And when I honestly looked and saw that my kids and husband have been able to do it and my family did it, then I wondered how much more would anyone else be able to do it? I wanted to believe people are good-natured and have other's best interests at heart. But I looked back on my life and all the things they did and I knew that often that was not the case.

Over and over again, I had believed that this person would help me, that person will care, this person will keep me safe...I mean, they are the pastor, the police officer, the teacher, etc. They are supposed to help people; that's their job. But time and time again, they didn't help me. They hurt me. They used me. They abused me. They made it worse. And I hated it. I felt so helpless. So ashamed. Like I must have done something to make it happen. It was somehow my fault that the police officer's private stick was in my mouth. I felt like it was my fault that he was getting me to suck on his stick. I use the words "getting me" because I guess I don't know that I felt forced. I felt like I had to though because he had listened to me. He had taken the time to hear what I had to say, so I guess I felt like I owed him? I also didn't even really think twice about it. He pulled out his cock and I got down on my knees. It was as simple as that. And I do see how twisted that is to have honestly believed that...but it was easier to believe that than to the alternative--that there was really no one to help me at all, that they were all in on it and it was really me up against the whole world.

I mean, that's a pretty big thing for a little girl to bear on her shoulders and the psyche break hit eventually. Trying to keep it all together was an immense weight on me and the confusion and what was what tormented me. It manifested in relentless nightmares, night after night. I could only sleep during the day and it was short and fretful. It was bad that I was sleeping in the day and I was going to get in trouble for it but I needed to sleep. It was safer to sleep on the bus on the way to school and on the way home with my backpack on my lap and my arms wrapped around it to keep anyone from stealing it, than it was to sleep at home in my parent's house at night. I was terrified to be there but I lived there, I had to go back there. I tried to get a student loan to move out onto campus even but my parents made too much money so I was denied a loan. I had to pay for my school and car. They'll say they helped because they put some money in a RESP for me. The money they put in plus the subsidy the government matched their money with only paid for my tuition for one semester of university, not even the books. I paid for the rest through working and scholarships/grants. I was stuck living at home in that hellhole because I didn't have any more money than for that and I was single-minded in my focus to get a degree where I could help others.

My parents will say they helped by letting me live and eat for free at their house. They'll say that they financially aided me as well because they sold me their car for cheap. They held that one over me too. They said it was a really expensive car and told me they pretty much gave it to me. The facts are though that my budget was $5000 and they wouldn't let me buy any used cars that I found because they were "worried" that I'd get scammed. They knew nothing about used cars though. I feel like I got scammed by them because a couple months after buying their car, I had to pay $2000 in repairs on it or it wouldn't drive at all. They blamed it all on me though. And I believed them. I was a bad driver; I had heard the stalls I had made. It must have been me. They'll insist that they were the good guys though because they let me make payments on the car and paid for driver's education for me…I'm not sure they paid full price for it though.

I wonder what discount they got for it with the services I gave the creepy, old guy who I had driver's training with. I still remember driving along those windy city roads with him to who knows where. Trying to do it right, trying to understand what I was supposed to do and knowing that I was doing it wrong. I was freaking out, panicking. I was trapped in the car with this guy and who knew where we were. I was so scared that I worked myself up into a panic attack because I was so terrified that I would never get out of there. I remember feeling like I was going to fail the test/class and just so desperately wanting to get it right. I needed to get my license so I could get away from home as well as get to school and work. So, the driver's training guy was over top of me, his face in my face and I remember his short, almost army haircut, his creepy, old man beard, his pepper and salt hair and his wiry body build.

I remember being so scared of him and being turned on by him. I had this feeling of apathy stemming from this belief that I had to do whatever he wanted. So, I just blanked out. I forgot. I was just nervous. I wasn't a good driver. It was the hardest hill in town. Oh, the excuses I made in my head to just make it all be okay. Then I would go home and pretend that I was fine. I'd skip some meal cards or only have veggies or work-out for an extra 30 minutes. I'd punish myself because somehow, I felt that made it okay. How much better off might I have been living on a dorm away from them? At least then I wouldn't have been deluded that my room and board were for free. I wonder if I wouldn't have had my mental breakdown during university if I hadn't been so exhausted and afraid from trying to not be at home as well as trying to prevent it from happening. How naïve I was to believe that the lock on my door actually kept them out even though I knew that my mother kept the key above my door.

I told myself it was all my fault that I felt this way. Over and over my whole life they always told me it was my fault, explicitly and implicitly. It was my fault that I felt this way. It was my fault that I was crying. It was my fault they were doing this. It was my fault that I'd gotten the question wrong. It was my fault that they had done this or that or hadn't done this or that. They were never to blame—they told me they'd always loved me and tried their hardest and I was the cruel, impossible one, holding grudges, being overly emotional, taking up so much of their time. A good Christian girl forgives and forgets so I was urged to adhere to this ideology. They reiterated that they had said sorry which to them meant that I now needed to shut up, forget it and open up. I would be so confused because they had just told me that they were sorry and now they were doing it again.

They'd slap me and scare me, threaten, blame and confuse me and distort it until I didn't know what was happening really anymore because how could this happen if they loved me like they said? How could this happen if they were sorry like they said? There were always their reasons to excuse their behavior usually blaming me. They'd blame me for their actions citing that I'd taken so long to tell them, cried too much, made them stay up late listening to my sob story and so forth. They always left out the full truth such as that while I may have made my mother stay up late because I needed to talk, it was her who kept us up even longer. She would listen to me tell her about some of the things I was struggling with, made me feel like she cared and then got me to comfort her in the ways she had taught me to relieve her. Why was she the one who needed comfort? She needed comfort because I got hurt? Why wasn't I the one being comforted? Well, I was being somewhat comforted comforting her and I guess I felt good too but I felt gross and used and dirty too. I lied to myself though and chalked my inner pain up to being from what that boy had done instead of seeing how much worse what she was doing to me was. I lied to myself that I felt okay. It didn't matter how I really felt or how manipulated I was; it was just all about them.

During the healing, it was overwhelming how confusing it all was. I don't know if I can really explain how confusing it was. And how alone I felt. How full of despair and eventually, apathy I was. There was no point in fighting it because it just made it worse. It was better just to shut up and take it. It was safer to lie to myself that I was okay than it was to fight it, make it much worse and still have to do it. And I have felt like this an as adult, as a mother and wife. My husband and son were good examples of this before my husband was able to let go of some of the trauma ruts from his past that he was stuck in (and my son was his copycat because I was a doormat) and before I was able to say no to the abuse. They cared so much about these things and I just didn't want to fight about it. Why did it matter? I would submit and do what they wanted with little to no regard for what I actually wanted. I became so entrenched in this belief that I was actually happy if I was doing what made others happy that I didn't see the wretched prison I had created for myself.

I didn't want to stand up and demand respect. I wasn't willing to risk rocking the boat and early on in our marriage, we both were too unhealed for that to have been a safe choice as well. There was also the psychological abuse to sift through. My past repeated itself in my adult life where I would be berated by my husband for doing one thing and then when I would change it, he would then beat me down again for doing the exact thing he had said he wanted me to do. We were stuck in that cycle for the longest time because that had literally been the story of my life. I was always "damned if I did, damned if I didn't". Living in that constant state of…um, confusion, torment?? It ate away at me inside with this gnawing, aching, relentless itching.

Eventually, I got really tired of living that way. I no longer just wanted to not be stuck in those patterns of past guilt and shame, I made conscious changes to break free from it. Some days, during this healing journey, it felt like those programs ran me. That they were me. If I wasn't run by guilt, fear or shame, who or what would I be? I was haunted by a past I couldn't erase and further, I was bound by a prison I couldn't even see. I felt like I did not know how to break those chains or free myself and I felt like I was drowning in this pain and this fear. Sometimes I wondered if they were right. Was it just me? Was I just a screwed-up mess? Sometimes I even wondered if everyone would just be better off without me.

I don't write this to make anyone feel bad for me. Honestly, for a long time I felt too ashamed to write this. I wondered what people would think of me knowing how I've felt. But I want that person out there who feels like I've felt to know that they are not alone. You deserve to heal. You are still worthy. You are important and good enough to take up space. Sure, you're not perfect and you've got your shit to work on, but you're not the scum of the earth, garbage on the bottom of their shoe that they want you to believe you are. You see, as long as you're beaten down, they get what they want. As long as you don't believe in yourself, they can do whatever they want. And they will keep pushing and pushing, pulling and demanding that you give until you feel like there's nothing left. And somehow, you'll still feel that shame and keep giving until you choose to heal that past pain.

And does that make them a bad person? I don't know. I'm not here to pass judgment. As a child, it was never our fault. As adults though, as long as we are walking around blaming everyone else and feeling like a powerless victim, are we not asking for this behavior, this self-perpetuating trauma cycle to continue? At the same time, if someone knows your traumas and consciously uses them against you, are they not taking advantage of you, using and exploiting you for their own gain? But again, this isn't about who should pay or whose fault it is or even who the so-called bad guy is. This is about looking at the intricate layers and trying to make sense of a multi-dimensional thing while expanding the limitations of the traumatized mind. We cannot control anyone else. Our only "control" is in getting to know ourselves, going deep into the depths within, into the pain and the dark crap and healing and growing from within. We give all our power away when we say it's so and so's fault. We gain everything by accepting true responsibility, letting go of that which we cannot change and going deep within to transmute all as it bubbles up.

Chapter 4

This Little Flicker of Light

I remembered him with every fiber of my being. I felt him before I saw him and every part of me came alive. It was that ultimate feeling of coming home and I knew that I belonged. I felt the safest I had ever felt and that feeling that everything is going to be alright washed over me. I had this feeling of floating on air. And he saw me and he knew me and I was whole once again. It was like that piece I had been looking for, that part that was lost, was found. When I remembered, I wondered how I'd forgotten. He told me how they'd erased my memories. He told me how I'd been having a hard time and that I'd been so traumatized by what they were doing that I wasn't keeping it together enough for them. So, they'd erased my memories and in doing so, they took him, my everything, with them. From age 4-8, they took them all away. They stole him from me.

My, I don't know exactly what to call him, was he my older brother, my best friend, my boyfriend, my twin flame, my other half, my imaginary friend, my divine masculine, my guardian angel, my soul, my inner child, my intuition, inner voice, me? I don't know. I just know what he meant to me and what he did for me. You see, every time they hurt me, he was there to comfort me. When they abused me and shattered me into pieces, he wiped my tears and stroked my back. When I was covered in their filth, he helped me clean up, dried me off and warmed me up. He held me while I threw up from what they had done. He iced my wounds and cared for me. When I was afraid, he comforted me. He pulled me onto his chest and stroked my hair, holding me close so I could feel safe. He was my one solid thing. I always thought my grandfather was the one I loved most in my childhood but it was this whomever he is who I truly loved the most. And when they took the memories, they took him too and that was the day I truly lost so much of me.

When I saw him, I felt this warmth fill my soul. I was reunited with something sacred and monumental that had been lost. I don't think I can truly explain to you how it felt. It was so bittersweet. Then he was gone again but I still remembered this time. Healing came at a much faster pace after that. It was like it broke loose this dam and I just started really flowing forward. These kinds of moments happened every so often, my whole life, and they filled me with a kind of energy, hope even, to keep going no matter how dark it felt. They were the breath that comes just soon enough to stop you from drowning. They are the kind of moments that one could easily miss or just chalk up to nothing but I felt, knew even, that they were more. Maybe they were just dreams or hopings, you can call them what you want. To me though, they were gifts from the Universe to replenish and strengthen me along the way. They made me feel like I wasn't alone and there was something more than just this pain. So, no matter how hopeless it felt, there was always this little flicker of light that I held on to.

This memory came in two parts. The first part was just the skeleton. I was overwhelmed with the feelings of betrayal when I first remembered. I felt gutted that my grandfather, whom I adored, could do this to me. So, I could barely handle the basic outline of what happened. Later, I was able to see the rest. My grandfather bragged about the deal they got on their new, big motorhome. I didn't understand why it felt like a knife twisting in my gut until I remembered the way I'd helped them get that deal with the payment I had made in exchange for the amount they saved. I still remember that guy. He was pretty hot, athletic build, super short, military haircut, straight business, to-the-point kind of guy. Maybe 40, I don't know, I was a kid. I remember thinking I was helping them some other way until it was too late and I was alone in that room with him, up on that table naked, no real choice of my own. I remember him coming toward me and I was so scared and nervous but also turned on (I could feel the energy pulsing in my privates, tingling). I felt so betrayed and angry and then ashamed and mad at myself because I felt like this was my fault somehow. But it didn't matter how I felt because they always just got to do whatever they wanted anyway. So, I shut it out and I let it fade away, I didn't want to remember what he did to me that day. So, I went somewhere else and let my body do the rest.

Later, I looked at the memory more closely and I was able to remember more. I was all groggy, alone with this man in this small room by myself. I was lying up on some sort of table on my back. I watched in morbid fascination as he approached me, a mixture of excitement and fear, disgust and appreciation, repulsion and desire. To me, getting a better price on their motorhome was wonderful. I was so happy for them saving money on their big purchase so of course I'd been happy to help make that happen. No matter how many times it happened, there was still a part of me that was naïve enough to believe that this time it would be different. All I knew was that one minute I was playing with my Giga-pet--this cute, little, yellow Giga-pet with pink buttons and a little cat to take care of. Then suddenly I was waking up kind of groggy and alone with this strange man. It's no wonder I rarely played with my Giga-pet at home and how that little cat was always appearing on the screen wearing his halo saying I'd killed him with my neglect. Stupid little cat, stupid useless cat that just begs for more…food, water, attention, cleaning up after it…everything.

The man greeted me as he rubbed my cheek. I couldn't really speak; I could barely move. I couldn't move away from his touch so I just watched him wordlessly. I saw his short, pepper and salt hair, his military-like, athletic body. I was grossly excited and apathetic at the same time. He reached over, took off my shirt and then touched all over my chest. He grabbed my pee-pee through my shorts and growled in my ear. I lay still as he fumbled with my shorts button and then pulled them off, panties too. He looked a bit upset about that, I guess, because he pulled my panties off too. I knew that sometimes they don't like to do it all at once.

I watched him, my heart pounding in my chest, as he pried my legs apart and then slammed his hand against me and inside me over and over again. It felt amazing and it hurt and it felt great and it was painful because every time he slammed his hand back down it smashed my pee-pee and it hurt on the outside. Eventually it just hurt, all of it. And he didn't care; he didn't quit until he was done. Then he suddenly stopped and moved to the end of the table. He grabbed me by the ankles and slid me down to the edge against him. And I lay there as he shoved himself in me over and over. I just waited until he was done, praying it wouldn't be long and hoping that that was all that was left before I could go.

I felt so ashamed and betrayed as I picked up my clothes and put them on. I stumbled out of the room into the bright sunlight, blinded by the sun. And I blamed the sun for my tears. My family asked me how my nap was as if to save face to the people around, as if that was the reason I was stumbling around and not the horrible pain in my private parts. I felt like there was this heavy rock in my stomach and I felt like I just didn't want to remember. But I knew they will always remember because the recorder was on the wall and it watched it all happen. And I knew that they all could see it whenever they want. I watched my grandfather pull out his wallet and exchange money with the man who hurt me. They laughed together like they had this special little joke. I just wanted to die but I couldn't. So, I faked that I was fine and lied to myself pretending that nothing ever happened. It was just a nap.

You know, I have always wondered why the movie *Sucker Punch* spoke to me so much but I see now that I did that very thing that Babydoll, the main character, did to survive. She would retreat to a fantasy world in her mind while the abuse happened and it would protect her from the harsh reality of what she was facing. For me, I just slipped away into this gray fog, this place where I was there but I wasn't. I felt everything and yet I felt nothing. I experienced everything but I remembered very little right afterwards. It was a place where everything they did was dampened and I could handle it. And through it all, I held on to this hope, this little light inside. I begged and prayed that this pain I was going through would one day help someone else. At that time, I didn't know how or what exactly I would later do but all I wanted was that the pain I experienced be able to ease someone else's pain. I felt so alone and I didn't want anyone else to feel like I did. So, I vowed to myself that I would do what I could to help other kids and hurting people and I would not give up the fight. I would hold on no matter how dark it got to that inner light and one day, I would turn it into a blazing fire to light the way out for those who couldn't see it for themselves.

Sometimes the fear has crept in. And sometimes I just wanted to forget. From time to time, I have felt like I don't have a choice because I have just forgotten sometimes. I have felt like I have no control over the healing process. The memories come up when they come up and they affect me how they affect me. Occasionally, they have hit me like a punch in the gut and other times, it has been this big relief to just have it out. Other times, I have felt completely fine and then I would slowly unravel over the next few days. I wasn't always in tune with what was going on with me. That in turn would sometimes escalate into me being mistreated in my present day because my husband would pick on my unhealed energies and our unhealed traumas would do their toxic dance. Then every now and again I would kind of "lose" that traumatic memory I'd recovered because this new trauma would be there but in reality, they were both there.

I would be overcome by these layers of trauma while this hammer was being held at me that if I didn't do better, that would be it. It was the story of my life. It was always my fault. I was always never enough. It was a long time of dark struggle and trying to pull ourselves out of the entanglements of the past. How we were able to heal this far and grow together on this journey despite the traumatic and dark struggles we went through together and growing up had a lot to do with a determination (particularly on my part) to push through. I firmly held on to a belief that we would be able to heal and eventually work together as a team, not just be two traumatized people who continually bled on each other. More so though, I believe the Universe put us together because we were exactly who the other needed to heal, learn and grow.

There were times when I allowed myself to be the verbal punching bag. I'm the first one to admit I'm not perfect and that my husband and kids all deserved me to be better so at the end of most arguments, I was the one accepting fault and blame far beyond what was mine to truly carry. I already felt like the dirt on the bottom of someone's shoe so it wasn't hard for me to accept the role of the family scapegoat and maid. At times, I had clarity and recognized that what was being said was about me and it was not about me. There were moments when I was able to see how badly I had been abused my whole life and felt so much grace towards myself. How could someone so traumatized and being traumatized actually be expected to be doing any better than I was? And it was these glimmers of light that kept me going when the darkness threatened to take me under. Even as I couldn't stop the shuddering sobs from leaving my body and held myself back from the edge by barely a thread, there was this steady, beating drum that kept me going forward when all around me I felt like they were cheering for me to give up.

At times I've wondered why I was letting this past pain get to me. What good did being gutted by the latest memory serve? But I couldn't really stop the pain from coming in sometimes. And I do think it also deserves a place to exist, at least for a time. That pain was real and that little girl was really hurt. She had no safe place to talk about or feel that pain and that pain needs a voice, a time to have its stand. And so that's another reason I'm writing—to give this pain a place to live outside of my body. I carried it for so long and now I've chosen to set it down. It was dragging me down. I was allowing it to suck the life and joy out of me. There were times when I felt that perhaps I wouldn't ever find that beat in my step or that deep, belly laughter again. I felt trapped in a sea of fear, pain, shame and despair. Over time, the shame decreased but that baseline of shame, it was very hard to shake. Over and over, I revisited it and I could see in my mind that it was not my fault; I was a child. And then over and over in my heart I felt like it was my fault and I should've, would've, could've. And we went around and around, those two opposing sides. I felt helplessly stuck like a hamster in the hamster wheel. I was running away, I was running toward, I was running away, I was running toward.

A part of me didn't want to write because I was worried that if it was known how I have felt sometimes that they would say that I am not a good enough person to be a mother. I could hear in my head over and over all of them shouting that I was the problem, the one who was in the wrong, the one who deserved all the punishment and pain. All the times being threatened with the us versus you rhetoric echoed in my head. All those times they blamed me and said that if I had had a backbone and had stood up for myself and what I wanted, that this wouldn't be happening either reverberated in my mind. And it was over and over, my childhood repeating itself and it was like I was stuck in this infinite loop where I was the insane one though who somehow thought the next time over this loop the end result would be different even though we were on our five hundredth time around. But there were little changes and things were never quite the same. So, I had lied to myself so many times that I was used to it being that way.

And then you get married and you have kids. The kids you dreamed of for years. Kids who would know what it means to be loved and accepted for who they are. Kids who would be intelligent but also compassionate. Kids who would know how to have a friendly debate and walk away from it "losing" and still know their self-worth. Kids who would be able to compromise and work out conflicts with others. Kids who would problem-solve and who weren't afraid of failure. Kids who would be provided a safe environment where they would always know that they were fully accepted, loved and wanted. Kids who would have a dad who would care about them, appropriately play with them and truly see them. Kids who would be encouraged to be independent but also not be expected to carry the weight of the world on their shoulders.

And then reality hit. Two weeks in and suddenly, my newborn son started screaming. It felt like he never stopped. His screams and cries scraped over and over on the unhealed wounds from my childhood. All those times I had cried out for help, sobbed in fear and screamed in pain were now being awoken anew with every tear he cried. I didn't know what to do. He always demanded and demanded and took and took. It didn't matter how much I gave; it was never enough. My husband thought that a kid wouldn't cry if you gave it all the love and so he thought there was something wrong with the baby or me or both of us. And it was always my fault. No matter what I did, my husband blamed me. I felt like the baby blamed me. I blamed me. I was still around my family at the time and well, they blamed me. They would tell me that my picking him up was spoiling him. They would question the quality of my milk. They would say it was this or that that I was doing that was causing his crying. My mother would send me memes written from a kid's perspective saying that they were going to her house because their mom was "crazy" or something similar. The message always the same—you're the problem, the one causing your kid to cry...it's all your fault.

There was no support, no offering of help, no solidarity at 2am in the morning for the 525th day in a row. There were usually wide eyes and faces of horror when I would tell people of how little sleep I got and how much the baby and toddler screamed and cried. But no one really cared because no one was ever there. They were just happy it wasn't their kid. You might be thinking that it was colic or teething. He checked out just fine with the doctor. And sure, I made a lot of excuses for it such as teething. When those excuses seemed hollow even to me, I moved on to excuses like jealousy about sharing me with the new baby, toddlers have a hard time with no's, I just need to explain it to him more and one day, he will grow out of it. Maybe there was some deeper reason, perhaps on a spiritual level. Maybe he and I were doing this intricate dance and he was reacting to my inner pain. Maybe he was meant to do that to show me just how demoralized I really was that I allowed a little kid to run me.

Most likely, it was a combination of many things. What I do know though is that my unhealed traumas thoroughly impacted our relationship and our family. My inability to say no, nonexistent boundaries and deplorable self-esteem wreaked havoc on our home. I wasn't able to truly parent because I didn't respect myself therefore, I couldn't garner his respect. Many years of struggle later, it took some brutal honesty to finally come to this realization that I had a husband and growing child who were both throwing tantrums because I had set the precedent that my no and I meant nothing. And that's another reason why I'm writing this because hardly anyone talks about how those tendrils from the past wrap themselves around you and cinch themselves tighter and tighter until you can barely breathe and you hardly can tell where one starts and where you end.

I guess if we look back on it, saying no has always been hard for me. Frankly, it wasn't even until recently that I realized (maybe I don't even fully now), all the things I have a right to say no to—and simply because it is my right. I wasn't taught to say no though and actually was taught that saying no was almost like a sin. There were a lot of punishments for saying no. I didn't even have to say no…I could just look like I wasn't excited about it or I wouldn't say yes or start doing it fast enough and a hand would be around my hair and then they'd be screaming in my face that I had better start behaving or it was going to get a lot worse. If I started to cry, that would only infuriate him more and he'd start to lose it. She would give me this look and I'd know I'd done it now. And I would slowly fade into my place of safety, the gray fog that kept me alive, although devoid of a lot of emotional depth, for so long.

Chapter 5

The Psycho Mother

I grew up with a self-implemented, very strict dress code, primarily due to what I had read in the Bible and other books. It wasn't until recently that I actually understood where the rest of it truly stemmed from. You see, we were a church-going family and the kind of church-going family who dressed up. And I wore dresses. Every Sunday, I wore a dress. In the fall and winter, I also had to wear horrid pantyhose that I hated because they were so itchy. At Easter and Christmas, there were special dresses. And never was I ever given a pair of shorts to wear underneath. No, I was taught that I must keep my legs closed and further, that I must cross my legs when I was sitting with a dress.

I don't know how old I was exactly, somewhere between the ages of 8 and 12 because of the house we were living in at that time and I was wearing a dress. I didn't sit appropriately; I sat with my legs open. My mother called me on it, pointing out what I had done. Instantly, I was filled with this sinking feeling. Shame and dread coursed through me. With no time to really think about it or even stammer out an apology, she started demanding I take my underwear off and sit in my dress with my legs open, now naked. I wouldn't do it. I was appalled and completely embarrassed that I would have to sit like that and have anyone look at my private parts. So, she came at me and I backed up to try and get away. But I was close to the wall in the kitchen next to the green china cupboard and quickly was trapped with my back against the wall.

I froze as she loomed above me. She took my panties off me. I guess I just kind of gave up. I was crying but eventually I stopped and just woodenly watched her as she did whatever she wanted. She took me and made me sit on the chair. She tied me to one of those wooden chairs we had from that kitchen table we had for the majority of my growing up years. I remember the way those chairs looked with the rounded wooden backs and the nicely shaped pieces. I remember the golden oak colour of them. I remember how much my parents had debated over getting that table and chairs because it was so expensive they had said. And how they had eventually bought it because it would be so perfect for our home and for homeschooling.

She tied my legs open so that I had to sit there with my pee-pee out. It was weird sitting on the chair like that. I was cool and I was embarrassed. I was afraid of what she would do next. I couldn't move and I thrashed against the ties once the panic set in but I couldn't get free. I stared at her in horror, hating her. Eventually she took my whole dress off and made me sit there completely naked in the kitchen, completely spread eagle, trapped there on that chair. She shrieked at me with insane words, twisted jabs, exerting her dominance. I just stared at her, mute. What was there to say to this psycho? At times, I recognized how just obscene their abuse was and other times, I thought that I deserved every punishment they gave. She left the room for awhile and then she came back. In her one hand she held a glue stick about a half inch thick by six inches long.

In her other hand was her video camera. I'm not sure which I was more horrified to see in her hands. She set the glue stick down and turned on the video camera. She put it to her face and squinted her one eye. She always looked so weird when she did it. Then, she turned it on and recorded me tied up there naked on the chair. I tried to move, I guess to maybe hide myself, of course to no avail. My heart was pounding and I could feel my cheeks burning with shame. And I stared at her. She brought the video camera slowly closer and closer to me and she squatted down right in front of my pee-pee with it. With one hand she recorded and with the other she touched me, my pee-pee. I could feel my pee-pee getting all funny and I was mad at myself because I knew how much they always liked that. I knew somehow that it looked different when that happened and I was angry that I couldn't make myself stop. She set the video camera on the table and looked through it, I guess so she could make sure it was lined up so it would record what she was going to do next.

Then, she took the glue stick that our pastor had preached to the congregation was the appropriate tool with which to punish your children (it would hurt a lot but it wouldn't leave any marks like a wooden spoon he had said). She took the glue stick and she drew with it around my naked body. Around my nipples, down my arms, across my belly, down my legs, then back up my inner thighs. I shivered. Maybe I was cold, maybe I was reacting to the touch. She circled my pee-pee (vulva) then slowly dragged the stick up and down from the chair seat all the way up my pee-pee then back down again.

Up and down, up and down. She murmured words of pleasure at me while she swirled it over and around my pee-pee. It felt so good that I started to think that maybe this wasn't so bad after all. I mean, it was really embarrassing but it also felt so good. I was so confused--I was in trouble and now this felt good. I was trapped there and there was nothing I could do. And I absolutely hated that feeling. I wondered who might walk into the kitchen and see me there too and I wondered what they would do to me too. I was feeling nervous, dizzy, like I was going fuzzy and grey around the edges. I had no idea what she was going to do next.

Then, suddenly, she whipped my pee-pee with the glue stick. I screamed. She held her hand over my mouth so that my screams would be quieter, I guess. She whipped me over and over, all over my pee-pee, across my thighs, over and over again. I felt myself struggling against the ties and it rocked the chair. I guess that made her mad because she shoved the chair back until it was against the wall. She shoved it so hard and fast that she slammed the back of my head into the wall. I was stunned and saw black and stars. I shook my head to try to clear it. I tried to reach my hand up to rub my head but I couldn't. So, I just watched her. I knew if I said anything, I'd just make her madder. Eventually, she shoved the glue stick up inside me and jabbed it back and forth.

It wasn't too bad. I'd had it a lot worse before. It kind of scratched at the edges but it was small so it wasn't that bad. Then, when she took it out, she whipped me again on the pee-pee with it and the legs which hurt even worse because it was wet. I looked down and I was all red and sore. I peed myself eventually at one point which made her even more mad. Then she took her pants off and shoved her hairy parts in my face and made me lick them. She thrust the glue stick in my hand and made me put it in her. I guess she must have untied my hand. It was a lot and it was hard to focus on all of it. Trying to lick and push the stick took all my concentration. I tried so hard to do it right hoping that she'd untie me and let me go then. Finally, she was done. I knew this because her wetness was all over me. I was relieved. Maybe she was going to let me go now. But she didn't.

She left me there, covered in her wetness, cold and shivering there. It smelled and my mouth felt all cottony and dry. It was hard to swallow. There were hairs stuck in my mouth and I couldn't get them out, her little, curly, brown hairs stuck tickling my throat. I knew better than to throw up though because she had made my brother eat his puke when he puked up creamed corn once. Eventually, I heard the back door open and shut and some keys jingling. And I knew it was my dad. When he walked into the kitchen, he didn't see me at first. When he did though, his face got his sick, happy look and he turned a bit red. He set the keys and the bag he was carrying on the counter. No words were exchanged. It was just these slow actions, slow-mo snapshots. Then he was over me and I found myself using my free hand to undo his belt and pull out his hard stick.

I rubbed it and then I put it in my mouth. I thought I was doing a good job; I was trying so hard. Honestly, I felt kind of okay because this somehow made me feel better. But then he moved forward and slammed my head against the wall, his hard stick in my mouth, down my throat, choking me. And I could hear myself making these horrible sounds and I tried to get away. I slapped at him with my hand but it didn't matter. He released a bit and I had a flash of hope before he slammed my head back into the wall with his body, over and over again until he shoved it down my throat so hard that I couldn't breathe at all. And then suddenly, he backed away. He put his stick away, picked up his bag and keys and left the room. And so, I learned to sit properly like a good, little, Christian girl in my pretty, little, Sunday School dresses.

At the hospital/clinic earlier that day, it had taken many hours, four my mother had said, from getting there to leaving. I got to get a waterproof cast for the hairline fracture on my wrist, an upgrade, because of course I wanted to be able to go swimming and take showers easily, it was summer! Little did I know though of what I was agreeing to. She left me in that room, alone, with the doctor. She left me in there alone and let him do whatever he wanted. She didn't care that my arm was hurting, she didn't care what I wanted. I don't know that she even cared what happened. Either way, I paid for the upgrade then and I paid for it later when he came again. But I still beamed with pride and was so excited to show off my new cast to all the kids at church. The children's pastor even came over and signed it...and I never understood quite why I was so embarrassed and excited that he did so, except I remember now that what he drew on my cast, that some would say was a smile, was a penis and balls.

And I remember the closet, the small, dark room I went into with the children's pastor and I remember his pants unzipped, the hazy feeling and also the excitement and pride for being chosen by him. How I loved the attention! Normally, I felt so deprived of attention and so unwanted and here, I could perform and excel...and I felt that would maybe make me worth something. Maybe I knew it was wrong because it was a secret or maybe I didn't and I just knew that I didn't want to get in trouble for telling. But somehow the other girls always knew even though I never told. I did what he told me and I tried so hard to get it right. I was so scared and I was so excited. I just wanted to be a good, little girl and not get in trouble or lose my special job. If he cast me aside then I'd have failed and I'd have sinned. And I wondered if Jesus would still love me.

Looking back, I've wondered why I needed to take a shower after getting my arm cast. Sure, I'd gotten sweaty rollerblading but would it really have been that bad to push the shower to the next day? I mean, we had gotten me that waterproof cast and by the next day, it would've been set enough that I could shower with it. By having to shower that same night, I had to try and keep it dry. It seemed like such an unnecessary hassle. My mother said I had to shower though and so I did. I remember being so embarrassed that she was helping me. I didn't want her to help me but she told me that I would need help. I felt like I had no choice but to let her help me shower. I was 9. I told her to not look and she promised not to. Yet, when I got out of the shower and she was bent over helping me dry off I guess, she most definitely looked…I've always remembered her touching. She reached her pointer finger out and gently felt the straggly, little pubic hairs that were emerging from my pee-pee. I kind of moved back from her and felt really embarrassed, confused, not sure what to do, and to be honest, aroused. She told me she didn't mean to embarrass me.

And that was all I could remember. But lately, I've been able to remember more of it. You see, there are many reasons I might have needed to have that shower. Perhaps I needed to wash off from paying off the doctor at the hospital. Maybe I needed to shower because I needed to be clean and presentable, properly appealing, for how they might be using me later that night. Possibly, I needed to shower then so that she could use her excuse of having to help me because she wanted to see me naked with a cast.

Or perhaps the shower was demanded because she too wanted her payment for having been so gracious as to have sat with me for all those hours waiting for the cast. I'm not exactly sure how she justified it; I don't really understand it. I just know I really didn't have a choice. Whatever she wanted, that's what happened.

Her fingers didn't stop at stroking the hairs, no, her finger slipped inside me and her mouth was placed on my pee-pee. There was nothing I could do but experience what was happening and I did love the feelings pulsing through my body. Every bit about it physically felt so good but I was so embarrassed, confused and ashamed at what I was doing, at what she was doing, at how I was reacting and I just didn't understand why. She pulled her fingers out and they were all wet and gooey. She showed them to me and told me what a dirty girl I was. She wiped her fingers across my face and grabbed my hair, pulling my face down to her pee-pee. She held my head there and didn't let me go. She told me to start licking and threatened that I'd better do a good job. I tried to back away from her; I couldn't breathe. She wouldn't let me up. She had me bent over and she smacked my bare, wet bum and told me to do better, to stop flailing. She must not have been impressed with my performance (or maybe she was) because the next thing I knew, something was shoved up my bum. I think it was the handle of the toilet brush. I screamed against her and tried with no avail to move away.

It felt like she twisted the handle in my bum and jabbed me with it over and over for forever while she told me that this too was my fault because I was a dirty, bad girl.

She kept hurting my bum more with the brush handle with what seemed so much pain. I was sobbing and begging her to stop. She agreed with the condition that I make her cum. She let go of me and I fell to my knees, sobbing. She started to grab me by my hair again, threatening me with more punishment. So, I got up on my knees, pulled apart her pee-pee (labia) and started licking her hairy, wet parts. I shoved my fingers into her hole just like she'd told me to and licked as hard as I could. Finally, she almost like peed everywhere all over us and she made me lick it all up. I looked down and could see the blood on the floor and on the handle. I was horrified and I felt woozy. She told me to get back in the shower and I did, shaking. I vaguely remember getting dried off and into bed. It hurt a lot. My arm hurt and I lay so still with my arm on the pillow because it was swollen. And I tried to be quiet and be good and not get in any more trouble.

Chapter 6

Alone in the Swirling Abyss

Growing up, when did I ever feel safe to express my feelings and emotions, my words, my thoughts? I don't know, never? When I spoke, I didn't really speak the words I wanted to speak. Instead, I said the words they wanted to hear, the ones they trained me to say. I don't know that I remember a time as a child when I didn't filter my words to please those around, to not rock the boat, to keep myself safe, to protect someone. I spent a lot of my life not knowing what it means to have a voice or to speak my mind. I've had people over and over again in my life who've lied to me and told me they cared about me, loved me and wanted to help me and hear what I had to say. And then I'd speak and they'd dismiss it or they'd nod and look empathetic or they'd shame and guilt me for speaking and because I was so deeply entrenched in the guilt and shame, I wouldn't even realize what was happening--that they were doing the exact opposite of what they had said that they would do.

And then there I'd be again, up on the pool table or back down on my knees. Once they'd used, they'd leave or go to sleep and I'd be left there to clean up the mess, both physically and emotionally. Then, when I wasn't able to "pull it all together" the next day and work some miraculous changes by their magical thinking that somehow because they had graced me with a bit of their time, that mysteriously, all would be fixed, they'd heap on the shame and berate me for my emotions. Instead of them looking at the raw truth that all they'd done was lie about being supportive...oooh maybe they didn't lie, they were being supportive--to themselves, they were caring, about themselves, they were loving, to themselves, they were caring of someone's needs, right, their own. It was my naivete, or perhaps my desperation or delusion or confusion or abuse, that led to me believing that the words they spoke were about me. I wanted to hear them say that I mattered and that kind of thing made me feel okay inside so I heard what I wanted to hear. It was my foolishness, naivete and abuse conditioning that led to me going back again and again for the same traumatic abuse (albeit there was no actual choice about the abuse as a child but the believing they cared about me part was a choice). It was my attachment to not being okay any other way.

What are you supposed to do other than censor your words, censor your needs, censor your being if at every turn, anything other than that is opposed and suppressed by a force much bigger than you? How is a child supposed to stand up against an adult when the adult is more than twice their size? Never mind when it's two parents versus a child or the whole family versus the child? What are you supposed to do when you feel free and then they swoop in around the corner, grab you and lock you in a dark closet? What are you supposed to do when they know exactly which buttons to push to get you back on your knees? What are you supposed to do when they've programmed you to be so ashamed and easily guilted or played off of the programs others have already put on you? What are you supposed to do when every time you make any progress, instead of praise and support, there are ten statements of how you could have done it better? How are you supposed to make changes and improve when you continually get triggered, retraumatized and put back into a trauma state? What are you supposed to do when the other person doesn't get it so you then feel like you have to pretend it's not there?

Psychological abuse is real. It's dark. It's confusing. It's like running through a maze with a blindfold on. It's this deep, soul-gutting abuse with tendrils that threaten to squeeze every last drop of sanity from you. It was very confusing even as an adult. It was beyond an incomprehensible terror as a child. I totally get why I just shut down, repressed, blocked it all away. I've read a statistic that a large percentage of girls who've had documented sexual abuse will deny it ever having happened when later asked about it as adults. I get that--how was I supposed to cope with the sexual abuse if I could barely focus to make it through the day with day-to-day tasks such as schoolwork, chores and church? Added to that was the invisible chores list of how to be or not to be as well as the long list for sexually pleasing them, emotionally pleasing them, mentally pleasing them.

Do you understand the stress this puts on a child? How is a child, now an adult, supposed to come out of a state of such utter terror, anxiety, confusion and dismay? Imagine that child holding this belief that eventually, as an adult, that's when it'll all be okay, someone will love me and take care of me, I will be safe and secure, I won't have to be afraid anymore, I can rest easy knowing we will get through things together. It was part of the hope that got her through those dark nights. So, the betrayal and gutting that was felt when instead of that, she was stabbed in the heart over and over with these lies and arrows of pain and twisted words, confusion, guilting and shaming and the yelling and the traumatizing and the re-traumatizing. Healing on your own in one incredible feat. Healing together, with another childhood abuse survivor and traumatized partner, is another thing altogether. There was this constant dance, this intertwining of pains, the way we bled on each other, the way his traumas fit so perfectly with my traumas that we just kept that sick cycle going and going. It felt like we would take one step forward and then three steps back sometimes. And sometimes his progress stunted mine (and vice versa) and we would get hung up because we weren't progressing together. The old patterns would come back to unconsciously try and pull the other back instead of rising together.

I became so sick of having to perform and yet I was so addicted to performing. I wasn't even sure that I knew how I could even stop performing or accepting punishment for not performing. I mean, there were a few certain things I just wouldn't perform and do and the ensuing punishment was totally worth it. Most other times though, the performance was perfectly acceptable, desired even, and so convincing, even to myself. But it started to wear thin. I just didn't know how much more I could "fake it 'til I made it". If I were to just let go of all of these fears, the worry was that there would be nothing to hold on to. There would just be free-falling, right into empty space. And apparently that was terrifying, more terrifying, than the current way of life for the longest time because I found it so difficult to change!

But I truly felt like I didn't know how to stop performing and obeying. I felt like I couldn't see what was standing up for myself and what was being a push over. I felt like I couldn't release the shame and feelings of it being all my fault. I felt like I needed punishment, I craved it even. Alan Watts says that the ego is the brain's siren going off about the dangers and alerts. He goes on to say further that we've been programmed to listen to it, follow it and jump when it says jump. And he posits that if you're doing that, how can you be anything but in a state of complete anxiety? And sometimes, I've felt like I didn't know where to put my next step. I didn't feel like I knew what ground to seek and then suddenly I'd be free-falling except I was resisting and so then I was hitting the branches and roots and rocks sticking out from the mountain.

For as long as I can remember, I've been trained to keep it all in. The last thing I wanted to be was a tattletale. It was a heinous crime in my family to spill the beans. When something happened, the status quo was to forget that it had ever happened or at least you better do a damn good job pretending that it didn't happen. So, imagine the displeasure and disgust as well as the guilt and shame cast my way when I developed an eating disorder, when I couldn't control the anxiety, when I started self-harming. "How could I bring such shame upon this family!" was the biggest message I received from my family right alongside with "you better freaking straighten your crap out right away before your problems tell everyone the truth about what goes on in this family". It wasn't necessarily said outright but it was implicitly said, over and over again in all the nuances only an abused child would understand. There was always a story to stick to and to defy that was to risk the wrath of the family cult. And luckily (or strategically done) for them, I was surrounded by other like-minded people who also wished to perpetuate this sick cycle of abuse so when I did indeed speak out about what was happening to me, I was met with the "stiches given to snitches".

In other words, what's a girl to do when her teacher, pastor, police officer, and neighbor are all in on it too? And man, do they really ever get their rocks off on punishing the snitch! Sometimes they did play the empathetic part, with a bit of comfort and we will call it, scraps of attention. And then they would just stab me in the back with what was said. They'd twist it and manipulate it for their own gain. They'd turn me right back into the hands of those I was snitching about but not until after they'd reaped the full benefits of being my confidante. I mean, what sick fun it must be to be the comforting confidante--a trained sex slave sure gives appreciative head to the man who seems like he cares about the horrible things that have happened to her and will do something about it. Imagine getting to play the hero. And then imagine the sick pleasure of then turning into the villain. Imagine watching the horror and then apathy on her face when he does do something about it--by pulling his belt off instead of doing it up after the thank-you blowjob and starting to beat her. Imagine his power trip as he loops the belt around her neck, tightens it and then yanks her up by the belt. As it all starts to get fuzzy as the pain around her neck increases and the oxygen to her brain decreases, her hands frantically and uselessly pulling at the belt to loosen it, he pulls down her pants and rapes her.

All that is reinforced in that moment. That feeling that all she is good for is to accept whatever punishment or treatment that is dished out. That sinking realization of how much worse she's now made it. Imagine being told by everyone around you that it is all your fault that this is happening and you really should have just kept your mouth shut. Well, sure, you can open it to receive the next one but that's really about all you're good for. You're a great sucker though. Imagine the confusion a young girl faces with that kind of conflict. Makes it pretty hard to ever trust again or want to speak the truth. It makes it seem much safer to live in a land in her head where those things don't occur. After that twisted psychological abuse, now imagine her being returned home to only be met with the narcissistic rage of two childish parents with zero self-control or restraint where she woodenly takes off her clothes herself before the door has even fully shut.

No real thoughts there, just this dark, empty pit in her stomach, the swirling in her head and the slow fade into the safety of the fog that has kept her as safe as she could be. As their actions become only a distant cacophony, she drifts into a place she created for herself. Dax calls it the abyss. And later though, after she's left them, she's lived so long in this abyss, she didn't know how to bring herself back from it. The horrors of what she's seen and experienced left scars on her that she didn't know how to loosen. They were hard lumps of tissue and she struggled to break through them, to loosen them, to return to her flow.

Do you see now though why it has been hard for me to use my words? Do you see now though why I was silent? If my parents could do those things to me for speaking out, imagine what an entire system could do that is based on this kind of sick, perverse abuse? The last thing they want is for someone to snitch. But I'm tired of being a coward. If I have to take another one or two or three, well, it wouldn't be the first time and you freaking know that this time I won't be silent about it. I know that there is nothing that can stop my truth, the truth from getting out. When I was a child, I believed my parent's lie that to forgive means to forget. I believed them when they got to pick and choose that which they chose to be the story of what happened and what did not happen.

I believed that things that had happened could pretty much be erased. I am no longer that naïve, little child and I know that it is forever written--every action, every count against an innocent child. Every violation will never be able to be erased. People may say it is forgotten but the truth is the truth and when you realize this, it really does set you free. You see, as long as you believe that this life is all there is, they have all the power. It is when you let go of your attachments though that you can step back into the seat of consciousness and find your true flow. And so, I've come to this place where I don't even know that I could choose to not speak out. It would just come out in one way or another.

I don't remember exactly when I gave pretty much all of it away save for that glimmer of a spark that was always there. Maybe it was when she looked at me with the "if looks could kill" kind of look and I knew what would happen later if I didn't change my behaviour. Or maybe it was when I realized that it didn't matter if I changed my behaviour or not, I was going to get it later anyhow. Maybe it was when all of them stood over me spitting on me, laughing at me, watching me splayed there with no where to go. Maybe it was when I swallowed for the 100th time. Or perhaps it was when I washed for what felt like the 1000th time and the smell wouldn't come out of my nose.

Maybe it was when I couldn't sleep and then I couldn't stay awake and then I wasn't sure which way was up or down anymore. Or maybe it was when the fear of the night terrors kept me awake until I succumbed to sleep and was terrorized by them again. Or maybe it was when I couldn't tell the difference between the terrors in my dreams and the horrors of my reality. Or perhaps it was when the blood poured down my legs from the self-harm and even that wasn't enough to make living bearable. Maybe it was watching her back as she abandoned me again…or when I saw her standing there, watching as he raped me and realized she'd never actually protected me.

Maybe it was when he took the truth, twisted and skewed it over and over and then got them to stand beside him and agree and I saw that if I didn't get on my knees, he could write whatever narrative he wanted, just like every one before him. Maybe it was when I realized that almost everyone just cares about themselves and their own lusts and that pretty much every person who I thought cared about me wanted me for one reason and one reason alone. Maybe it was when I realized that after they'd gotten me to give, they'd throw me out like the trash when they were done with me. Maybe it was when the demons screaming in my head began to flit in and out of my physical reality.

At some point, I almost lost it all, that small grasp on my sanity. I lied to myself that I could hold it all together forever. As the holes started to be blown through all the walls I'd put up to lock it all away, it unleashed this deep beast of emptiness, of darkness, of utter confusion and apathy. The terror that had always been clawing at me...once unleashed, it took over—not all the time, but it threatened to swallow me whole. I felt the claws around my throat and they squeezed tighter and tighter. With each word they said, every name they called me, every truth they twisted and used to drag me lower because they were afraid, because they too had been victims and didn't know any different, I felt myself shrink, becoming smaller and smaller. At some point, the most basic of tasks became hard tasks. The good cook burnt more food than not...someone who never burned food before. The shadow I had been to begin with faded even further and I became a mere wisp of smoke in the air. And it happened so slowly that I didn't even really notice.

The first time I remember riding the pony I was about six years old, lying in my little twin bed in the old Stoneybrook house. I would ride my stuffed bear, ironically cream-coloured and named Creampuff (such an interesting name as I don't remember eating actual creampuffs or even knowing what they were until I was about 13) until I was all sweaty and felt good. I'd do it over and over again until I couldn't do it anymore because I was too tired, it just wouldn't work another time or because I heard someone nearby. I remember hiding in my room doing it when no one was looking. I was ashamed that I did it. I didn't want anyone to know. I did not even really know what I was doing. I just knew that it had to do with my private parts and my pee-pee but I had no idea what I was doing just that I really liked it, that it felt really good. And I couldn't really stop myself. I would become overwhelmed with the need to do it and I couldn't stop myself from doing it.

Even when out in public around others, I eventually started to find ways to get that good feeling, such as crossing my legs and squeezing a few times to get that good feeling. Over my entire childhood, I remember really liking riding the pony and feeling really badly for doing so. One day, when I was around 10, I couldn't stop myself and needed to ask my mother, whom I sought for advice on everything, on whether what I was doing was bad. I felt very ashamed and like what I was doing was wrong but it felt so good, how could it be wrong? So, I finally worked up the gumption to ask her for the need to know overtook the need to not be embarrassed. She didn't seem surprised (which I thought was odd at the time) and just told me to try not to do it. And I felt like it was such a weird response because she'd given me a book on puberty which included masturbation (stating it was a sin).

When it came to organizing, I struggled. I didn't get how to keep things organized or straightened up. I was the kid with an armoire packed full with random crap that fell out when I opened the doors. I had a jewelry box jam-packed and every necklace some how was all tangled and knotted in what seemed like a hundred different ways. If my binders didn't have zippers on them, I lost my papers because the holes would rip and then I'd magically lose the papers. Later on, when I was really overwhelmed by the trauma (and pregnancy brain), the littlest of tasks seemed like monumental mountains to climb. I got them done but basic, ordinary tasks felt very overwhelming. It got to the point that if I didn't have a list, I couldn't seem to remember what it was that I needed to get done. Eventually, I was spinning around on fumes. All I could hear was the accumulation of all of them screaming at me and I felt myself slipping further away. I'd watch myself go and be helpless to do anything to stop it. Why are you saying this? Can't you see me here? I'm crying, sobbing naked on the floor.

How could you hit me? My nose was bleeding. Why didn't you care? I didn't understand. Then it was down my throat and I started panicking because I couldn't breathe. Why didn't you care? Why wouldn't you stop? I couldn't push away and I needed to breathe. I was desperate. I felt the blood spraying down on us. I felt myself hit the ground when he let go and heard him laugh as I fell. I curled up in a ball, trying to protect myself, hoping this would keep me safer. It hurts worse in the stomach. I was so cold. My nose hurt and the blood was still trickling out. I couldn't stop crying but at least I could breathe now. I startled as I felt his knees on my shoulders and tried to move but I couldn't. He was over me and he spread my legs. I felt his mouth on me. I couldn't stop myself; I felt my hips arching, my body moving as I felt the good feelings pulsating all throughout my body. As much as I was trying to get away, I liked it. I felt his fingers inside and I didn't want him to and I wanted him to and I felt so ashamed. I heard myself begging him in response to his words. As it felt the best, he told me what a good girl I was. I couldn't help feeling like a very bad girl though.

I begged for them to tell me what to do. I was desperate to do whatever they wanted. I just needed them to tell me what and how to do it. I wanted, no, needed to make them happy. If I needed to try harder, I would. If they wanted me to do it faster, then I moved quicker. If their desire was for me to bounce more, smile more, jump more, move more, entice them more or dance more, I was quick to acquiesce. And they would and I would. I was terrified of being alone, abandoned, shoved in the closet again. I couldn't handle criticism. Yelling traumatized me. I was used to walking on eggshells and that felt normal to me. It felt like everyone had hurt me. They just cared about my parts, my body. That's all that mattered to them and when I realized that, I realized I'd actually known that the whole time. I never mattered to them.

As long as I played the part and did as I was told, then I was allowed to exist. Exist is a good word. Perform is better. Play your part or get out. We will just cut you out and we will pretend you never existed because that's better than actually taking you as you are. Maybe it sounds pathetic to you. Maybe you get it. Maybe you find it disturbing. That need to be validated, to be wanted, to be cared for, loved, and belong exists in each of us and we all try (or at least have tried) in various ways to fill those needs. It's more overt with some and more covert with others. If you really think about it though, you can see it. The abused child trained to perform and valued only on getting it right becomes the overachiever, perfectionist, workaholic, doormat, victim, people-pleaser...a lost soul trying so desperately to be worthy of being here, of taking up space, of being seen and valued for as they are.

I just wanted someone to care. I wanted someone to actually see me. I tried in every way I could think of to show them that I needed them to actually care. But the cuts meant nothing to them. They just pretended that they didn't see them. They couldn't have not seen them. I purposely stopped hiding them in hopes that they would care and finally be there for me. And when my mother finally did say something, it wasn't to care. It was more to absolve herself of any responsibility and to be able to say she'd done her "due diligence" (although I don't know in what obscene, sick world she lived in where she could say that that was caring). First, she raided my room and cleaned it up while I was out (I was around 19 years old) and then brought out the items that she was upset that she'd found. She claimed having the right to enter and go through every one of my things due to the "risk of bugs" and lack of spoons in the drawer.

When I got home, she proceeded to shame me about what she had found in my room. She had found my cutting items though and chose to bring that up after she'd "shock and awed" me. With such disappointment, she questioned me regarding a desire to kill myself. I tried to explain that I was doing this because I want to live and the pain inside, I couldn't deal with. She didn't get it. She didn't even try. She just made it all about her. She guilted me over the sleep she would lose worrying about whether I'd be dead in the morning and threatened that perhaps she would have to take the door off my room. I tried to explain it further and when it fell on deaf ears, I suggested perhaps she should research self-harm.

She ran away and as I watched her back, as she ran away as if she were the teenager, I woodenly stared in fascination at this abomination. What had I just seen happen? I felt so utterly alone and unwanted. As I later stood over the toilet watching in captivation as the blood dripped into the water and then listened to the foaming of the hydrogen peroxide, I laughed a bit inside at how ironic it was that she somehow thought threatening to take the bedroom door off would do anything. But helping wasn't her intent anyway. I don't think she was capable of being truly helpful though.

This wasn't a part of her plan at all and she couldn't comprehend how to fix even a bit of the damage other than to shame and make a big scene to try to get me to change my behaviour that way. How would it look on the prestigious family if such a shameful thing was being completed, acted upon? We never spoke of it again. I battled that demon alone for the next few years until I closed that door. One day, after trying desperately to quit for so long, I was finally able to put down my blades for good. There were times that the pain inside got so great that I wanted urgently to cut again. But I white-knuckled it and despite the desire, I found healthier ways to let the pain out. My biggest motivation was my kids. I didn't want to set that example for them so I chose another way.

They just wanted me to shut my mouth and never speak of what happened. I was supposed to pretend it never occurred. They heard me cry...and they liked it. They heard me cry...and they didn't like it. Either way, they were sure to let me know that I was getting what I deserved. They blamed me that somehow I had asked for it. For it? What even was it? I didn't understand what was happening. I spent a lot of time wondering why they were doing this and why I was supposed to do this too. I would always find myself apologizing and accepting the blame. It was always my job to try harder and do better. I begged them to tell me what and how to do whatever it was they wanted me to do. I just wanted to do it right. Unlearning the very basis, the very fundamental program upon which my whole life was based has been one crazy journey. Shut up and do as you are told. That, I think, is one of the biggest underlying programs of this sick slave system, that and to be ashamed of being alive.

Chapter 7

Out of Control

I can barely remember a time where I wasn't self-conscious of my body growing up. There was a period of time where I wore only boy clothes...not because I wanted to be a boy, but because I wanted to do boy things and the clothes were better, particularly the pants. I liked the bulky cargo jeans and the loose slick pants. Looking back now, I no longer wonder why I felt this way. But I was naïve enough as a child to wholly believe that I was safer wearing those, though I would have whole heartedly stuck to the story that I liked the pockets on the cargo pants and how the slick pants sounded when I walked.

I had thought it was so great that my mother let me choose those clothes failing to realize that they just got to enjoy the tomgirl too. There was a period of time where I wore a couple dresses on repeat while pretending I was like a pioneer girl. I felt comfortable because they were reasonably long, loose and all the way up to the neck with long sleeves. There was also the season of turtlenecks because those felt cozy aka like a warm, protective blanket until those no longer felt safe because my nipples started to show through. Then when my nipples started to show through, I felt so embarrassed. The bras my mother bought for me didn't do anything to hide them and until she finally got me bras with real cups in them, I was so embarrassed.

By that point, I was developing hips as well as breasts and I felt so fat and embarrassed by my body. Swim suit shopping was the worst because she would make such a big deal about having to buy me separates because my bottom was so much bigger than my top she insisted. She would go on and on about how small my shoulders were and how tiny of a waist I had but my hips and thighs were much bigger. I guess she couldn't handle how my woman-like figure made her feel inside. She was a tall, boy-shaped woman so perhaps she just was unfamiliar with a developing, young woman's curvy shape or she just had such low self-esteem that she needed to try to knock me down a few pegs so she could feel better.

At that point, I started shopping for clothing at the old lady stores as a young teenager. I would wear old lady shorts and t-shirts in the summer with the shorts being almost to the knee and the shirts loose fitting with a high crew-neck cut, to be modest was my excuse. I also wore these jumpers that I asked my mother to sew for me. These were floor length jumpers that went all the way to the neck and I still wore a shirt under for "extra comfort". When I started to feel a bit "braver" I guess, I asked for a skirt, an A-frame skirt that went to the floor because I'd read that that would be a flattering style for someone who had such big hips as my mother had said I had. It was a beautiful skirt and I was so excited to wear it. She called me down to try it on when she was finishing it and insisted that I get down to only my undies.

Already embarrassed, things got worse because as she was measuring it on me, she made a big deal about the saddlebags I was growing. I didn't even know what she meant, I just thought she was saying I was fat in my hips. It was only a few years ago that I looked up what saddlebags are and further realized that what I have is just genetic and the way my hip bones curve. Yet with her one comment (it wasn't only that comment but it did stick), I spent over 15 years trying to get rid of them, something I can never completely get rid of. But it was something I would obsess over, focus on and still not be able to understand why I still had them even when weighing in at just a little over 100 lbs.

Even that underweight, I became even more obsessed with losing weight because I still had saddlebags so I must be fat.

Ultimately though, I didn't start out trying to lose weight or not be fat. I was just completing the hours for the physical education course I was doing from home which I think required some obscene 125 hours of physical activity. And for someone who was only moderately active before that, that amount of activity quickly made the weight fall off. And I wasn't overweight to begin with; I was just an average-sized 14-year-old. Then, at some point, I felt that it would be good to eat a bit healthier as well. That started innocently with cutting back on things like chips and sweets but very quickly turned into anything that contained any fat. I had zero knowledge of how the body worked and utilized food. I had no idea that my body required fat in order to function at that time.

When I was told that at one point in desperate attempts to get me to see reason and eat some food, I believed that my body could just use some of the fat it already had—like in the saddlebags and thighs. I was adamant that I did not need to eat anymore fat. I was certain that the saying "once on the lips, twice on hips" was true, for me anyhow, and that any fat I ate would go straight to my already fat hips and legs. I didn't understand that my organs needed a small cushion of fat around them to protect them. I didn't understand that some vitamins are only fat soluble so even though I was trying to eat lots of vitamins and minerals, I was still not actually absorbing enough vitamins and minerals into my body because I didn't have any fat. I got to the point that I was so low in vitamin K that when I'd wake up in the morning for school, I'd spend most of the time before the bus arrived with my head hanging over the toilet, blood pouring out of my nose. I would cry because I couldn't breathe, felt like I was choking and was terribly dizzy. I can still hear my mother berating me as she stood over and behind me while I was there crying and bleeding into the toilet for being so stupid to have caused myself to have this problem.

At some point along the way, the safe food options became smaller and smaller. First, it was only healthy foods allowed (whole grains, proteins, fruits/veggies, etc.), a pretty reasonable and healthy lifestyle, although a bit skewed with deprivation of the "fun foods" but otherwise pretty alright. But then the exercise increased and the amount of food allowed was decreased. Eventually, that didn't seem reasonable enough anymore so more foods became unsafe and then there were almost no foods with fat allowed. So, there was a lot of canned tuna, carrots and soup. The quest became to find high volume foods with very little calories; plain rice cakes, frozen applesauce cups and low-fat canned soups were my friends. It was a luxury to allow myself a ½ cup of low-fat cottage cheese but I accepted that that small amount (cue huge amount in my head) of fat was the acceptable trade off for the only 100 calories and 20 or so grams of protein (which I needed to make sure I could turn my fat, flabby legs into muscle!).

I felt like I was spoiling myself by allowing 1 tablespoon of peanut butter on my cut-up celery sticks—1 tablespoon spread ever so sparsely amongst as many pieces of celery as possible. I would freeze applesauce and pudding cups so that by the time I was eating them at school or at home, they would be slightly thawed and then I could ever so slowly eat them, helping me feel less hungry. I would make my food take such a long time to eat that I ate through a lot of my university classes…it was one of the ways I could help myself stay awake/focus/not hear the gnawing in my stomach; it was one of the only ways I could quiet Ana's voice in my head screaming that I was fat and should just fade away into nothing. As time went on, I developed other food phobias such as I could barely eat around others (save for when I was at school) but at home, I ate in my room by myself or at a different time. It was unbearable watching them watch me eat, seeing them count the mouthfuls and feeling the fat just pile on me with their gaze. Was I just packing all my anger away?

I eventually only ate a few things. I had a gruel I made and also considered my treat, which was plain instant oatmeal with a little salt, watered down so it was a very thin, runny gruel and then super hot so it took a very long time to eat. The same was for canned soups. I would water them down and heat them up really hot so they too took a long time to eat. Popcorn, plain and unsalted, was also a big hit with its low calories and high volume. Honestly, it seemed at one point that all I could think about was food and so to circumvent that, I found these ways to eat all the time. Failing to see that that was possibly making the problem worse, it didn't really matter because I was helpless to stop it (much like I was helpless to stop the abuse). Frankly, no one really seemed to want to help or cared how I was coping. All they cared about was that I was increasing my food intake and that the scale was going up. And with such a high volume of food and with it so hot, it was easy to make it look like I was eating a lot more than I was. At first, all I was trying to do was be a little healthier but as I got fitter, I just kept increasing the activities. I eventually started running on the treadmill in the basement with my boom box beside me, blaring the music on full volume while I ran, letting the words of the songs pound through me.

The Christian lyrics on repeat, over and over again, speaking of a God who was enough (and I was not) and of crying out to God to please hear me. I still know them by heart. What was it exactly I was calling out to? If only I had been able to see that it wasn't outside of myself I was seeking. If I would have seen that it is a part of me…it is me. I am the unseen. And there was always a reply, it just wasn't in words. I was never alone and of that I was always reassured. When I did walk away, I couldn't really say the reason why but I knew I wouldn't be coming back. I knew that this was the last time.

And that's one of the things I was most certain of in life, that I was never going back. I'd left a few times before but I'd always returned. But at that point, when I had my oldest, I was unwilling to subject him to that abuse. I couldn't do it for myself previously...I always went back because of the guilt, the shame, the conditioning, that belief that I needed them and wouldn't make it on my own. And that feeling that I deserved their punishment also led to me returning. But the thought of my son and my future children being subject to the horrors of my childhood was enough to cut through the fog, the self-doubt, the blocking of my intuition and I knew deep down that I couldn't stay in that toxic environment of my childhood family if I wanted to protect my kids.

I think my husband may be the only one who's ever actually loved me. For everything he's said, after everything I've said, after everything he's seen, he's still here, believing in me and championing for me, It was I who didn't believe in myself. For all the times that what he's said and done has re-traumatized me, it's been no worse than what anyone else has done. I was waiting for a hero on a white horse to ride in and save me when the hand to walk beside me if I was strong enough and believed that I was worth asking for it, was right there the whole time. But when I was just begging for him to see me as an object, to just tell me what to do, saying I couldn't do this...why did I expect anything else from him? Yet he was still there championing for me to stand up and do it.

What I couldn't see was that he couldn't do this for me. Every no, every lack of help, isn't the no...it's my opportunity to stand up, to try again, to be a big girl. But I was looking for someone to save me when it was me who needed to save myself. Christianity taught me that my help comes from outside myself, from God. So, I spent most of my life praying and begging for God to help me. When the help I imagined a God to give didn't come, I felt abandoned all over again. My family taught me that my help comes from them and then didn't give any help either. Society taught me to find help from a guy--he'll be able to save you, take care of you and keep you safe. Just do what he says and he'll keep you safe. Letting go of that belief and rising up into my own power has been both this heart-breaking and heart-warming experience. Looking back at all the ways I broke my own heart was a long-time hang-up until I chose to let go of my attachments to those experiences. When I learned to openly observe those experiences and actually learn from them, I let go of the shame for having demoralized myself. Rising up was then no longer an option...there were no other options.

For as long as I can remember, I wanted nothing to do with my father. I thought everything about him was gross--from the way his breath always smelled so bad, to the gross odor from the pimple cream he put on the acne he was so self-conscious of, to his creepy old-man sweaters-- everything he did annoyed, bothered or offended me. As a child, we would often take two vehicles to go places because he was on call. Sometimes, he wouldn't get called in so on the way home the option was to go with him and I would start freaking out at the thought of going in the vehicle with him. I would sob if I had to stay home with him. I remember him commenting once when I was wearing a lounge outfit on how nice I looked (I was maybe 11 at time) and I was quite upset with him. I felt so embarrassed and just wanted to crawl up under the floor or something so he couldn't see me. He would sometimes yell, though not all the time, and I would get so upset. I couldn't handle it when he got angry. I would start to panic, it would go grey around the edges, I would start to feel the floor fall out from beneath me, my breathing would increase, my head would start to hurt and everyone would feel so far away. He would purse his lips together really tight to the point that they would turn white. He'd get right in my face and I could see the spit flying out of his gross mouth with his gross teeth. And all I could think about was getting away.

Yet he knew I was motivated by money and he would pay me $20 to massage his knee and his toe. I mean, sure, why not? It wasn't for very long, it was a lot of money to a kid (like my whole allowance in one go) and I got to watch TV at the same time so it wasn't boring. Did I really get paid to ride the pony? Did he train me to ride the pony? Was I actually a paid child prostitute? Or a paid masseuse with special services? I always wondered why I felt that the TV was weird. It made me feel so funny watching the shows. Like hours could go by without realizing it and I'd feel so fuzzy and funny inside. I remember begging my father to help me with university studying. Could he please just help me practice the flashcards I'd made of the stuff I was learning? It was Biology so he should be familiar with it (but not that it mattered, I wrote the answers down). But he couldn't be bothered. Yet for my brother, he would spend hours on the phone. Then he would have the audacity to sit down and say that he didn't know why we had such a bad relationship despite him having read so many books on it. I think that's actually one of the most truthful things he's ever said to me though. Of course, he couldn't fix our relationship based on those books because his idea for making me feel special was to tell me what a good girl I was after I made him so happy riding the pony.

As an older teen, I didn't want him to look at me or touch me. I tried to repair the relationship later on as a young adult and he seemed at first to be trying to have somewhat of an interest in me for the first time in my life. We went on a few lunch dates, had some chats, etc. It soon became apparent that he didn't actually care about what I had to say and that the dates were more about his social status, his reputation, his ego…oh and less apparently but subconsciously very apparently, his dick. It got to the point that he would come (haha cum) visit my oldest child and I and it would seem that the visit had barely started and it would be time for him to leave. Interestingly enough though, he always had to bring me something. I can almost say for certain that he never came by empty-handed. If he didn't request a specific lunch order from me for some take-out place then he even went so far as to buy a 6-pack of expensive Starbucks muffins. Now, why does one have to bring something by in order to visit their daughter? Was he only just continuing the tradition of paying me for my services? And I thanked him in the way I'd been trained? I remember just cringing each time I had to hug him. I'd clench my fists and try to make it as rigid and little contact as possible. It must have been a laughing spot after all the contact we'd just had but hey, they gave me my little fit of protest, I suppose.

Growing up, I never wanted to ask for anything. In so far as if my dad would be stopping at the gas station on the way home and he'd ask if I wanted something, I'd always say no. I didn't want him to give me anything because I didn't want to owe him anything. I felt the same way in regards to Christmas and birthday gift lists. It first off, seemed so stupid; why would I want/need anything? Why would I want to look through the stupid Christmas catalogue and circle stuff I wanted? And secondly, no, I didn't want to repay for any of those things so I'd just say I didn't want anything. I'd always have to make a list though and gifts were always bought and payment was always made. What I missed out on though, was the fun of getting to pick whatever I wanted or perhaps leveraging my position into that of a position of power to get what I wanted in the transaction. I wanted to delude myself that if I didn't want anything or didn't willingly make the list, that then payment wouldn't be made. What I didn't see though was that all the while, payment would have occurred no matter what. My little child heart wasn't able to handle that truth though so it made up its unique story to keep it safe. Bravo, little one. You did so well.

And I remember hating the Christmas celebrations. I thought that the commercialization of it had made it a stupid holiday and I didn't want any presents, even as a child. I didn't want to make a list and I didn't want those decorations. But they made me wear the special outfits. They made me go outside in the snow. They put the cold snow all over my pee-pee so it was really cold and then they put the hot Christmas lightbulb on it after. They put it inside me and on my pee-pee and told me I better not move so the light didn't break and cut me. And I was so scared and I was so aroused and I was so confused and I was so tired or something. They would hold me open and stroke my pee-pee over and over again and I would pee myself. I would throw myself around. I was like this animal. It was so sick and embarrassing and I would do whatever they wanted. I loved that feeling. I needed to do what they said. It was all so out of control.

Chapter 8

My Choice

Every system I was in told me how to be and what to do. Say yes and do as you're told. "No" was not enough. They would make it clear that "no" was not accepted. If I said "no", they just pressed harder, hurt more or hit me where it hurt until I complied. As a child, what options are there really? You "die" or you comply. I don't necessarily mean die in the literal sense but more in the way the forcing of your compliance and obedience leads to a shrinking and shriveling up of you inside. I mean, you can protest but then there's punishment until you eventually comply. I didn't know about ways to get help. I didn't even really know that what I was experiencing was wrong. I fully believed when I was little that I was living in a safe, loving, Christian family…but as I got older, it became harder and harder to keep believing that lie. Their façade was something I started to see through. It would be much later before I saw through my own façade, the fake persona I had created that showed the world that I was okay when in reality, I was torn apart inside.

It was my job to make sure everyone was happy. One would tell me what was wrong about the other and confide in me. Then the other would do the same and there I'd be, loving him, loving her, being their parent. They didn't care to parent, to be the bigger person. I remember my father calling me when I was out on a rollerblade when I was close to twenty and he was saying that I needed to check on my mother and see if she was okay. I told him that she was not my problem. I was the one here having a hard time. I told him that I was the kid and that I needed help. I told him that I wanted to die and couldn't stop hurting myself. He didn't care that I wasn't able to sleep and was terrified every second of the day or that nightmarish, terrifying images plagued me whenever I closed my eyes. He didn't care about what I had just told him and reiterated that I needed to check on her because she was the one having a hard time. He was not concerned with how I was truly doing just as long as it fit inside his pretty, little image of what he wanted things to look like. I hung up and turned the music up…let everything burn, she walked away. Skating on, I was comforted inside by that internal realization that one day I would walk away; I'd truly drop a match and let it all burn away. Did I finish my therapeutic roller skate—was it therapeutic or was it a compulsion? I needed to control those feelings; this can get it out. Or was I skating because I believed that I was too fat and I needed to skate or run my fat away?

There's nothing wrong with exercising and I truly believe that as a part of a healthy lifestyle, exercise is necessary for health and well-being. But exercising because if I didn't the voices in my head screamed that I was too fat to even eat an apple is not exercising for health and well-being. Exercising because if I didn't, the demons in my head screamed so loudly that I couldn't even think. Exercising because if I didn't, I felt so ashamed of myself that I didn't deserve to live. When I was at that point in my life, exercising was not for health and well-being because I used it to punish myself. Exercising is not for health and well-being if it is a requirement for me to be allowed to go somewhere, do something, eat something, accept myself, love myself. Exercising is not for health and well-being if it is a compulsive have-to on the list of things to do with the goal to lose weight and get smaller so I can love myself. Exercising is not for health and well-being if it means that I feel ashamed if I don't exercise or stop ten minutes earlier than planned.

Exercising is not for health and well-being if it's about watching the clock to complete enough reps to feel adequate, worthy of living and deserving of taking up a bit of space. Exercising is not for health and well-being if it's the caveat for my worth as a being. Exercising is only for health and well-being if it compliments my life. It would be better to not exercise for a whole week than it would be for me to exercise for 20 minutes a day every day if it meant that the week without exercising, I did so because of the love and self-respect I had for myself. It took many years but eventually I reached a place of balance where exercise complimented my life and truly made my life and physical well-being better. I let go of the compulsion and found peace in moving my body in a variety of different ways that truly felt good to me. I learned to be okay with quitting a set physical activity because I didn't want to complete it or because I felt unwell…and I stopped punishing myself for not exercising or not exercising enough. I learned to trust the natural rhythm of my body. There are predictable times when I am more energetic and I don't force it on days when I need to slow down. I don't demand a work-out from myself after I was up all night with a sick kid like I used to. I don't feel the need to run for an extra half hour because I ate some French fries or a cookie anymore. I've reached this place where I trust my body to tell me what it needs…and now I actually listen.

I didn't reach this place of wholeness and self-love overnight. I spent years punishing and hating on myself—for what they did to me. I refused to truly look at where my pain was stemming from and stubbornly clung to false beliefs (i.e. I believed that my eating disorder was really just healthy living gone extreme…it wasn't). The shame that I was trained to carry was something I was so used to and dependent upon that I felt naked without it. The victim identity that I'd attached myself to was so familiar that I didn't even notice it anymore. Parts of me felt that if I forgave and let go, that they would all just get to walk away unpunished. After many years of self-harm, self-sabotage and self-defeating behaviours, I finally realized that this wasn't doing anything for me. I was losing more of myself every day and the ones I loved were being harmed by my lack of healing. I didn't want to set this kind of example to my kids. I didn't want to look back on my life and see that I'd given my abusers my whole life.

When I saw that my true power came from facing those terrors that happened, I started on that path and nothing could stop me. There were times I took detours and got sidetracked, but ultimately, I was steadfast on pulling myself up out of the ashes. That dream that little girl inside me had carried for so long, I reignited it. Her pain had a purpose and I wasn't going to join all those abusers and silence her any longer. No, I chose to choose her, to choose me. I chose forgiveness…and I found grace for me. Letting go didn't let them get away with it. It allowed me to find me and find my voice. Now my truth bubbles out in everything I do. I am no longer bound by the chains I locked myself in. I choose to live even when I feel like I don't know the way. This rising, this burning fire inside, I am breathing it in to every fiber of my being. What they tried to get me to give them, I finally realized that they could not have because I wouldn't give it away. And I found peace knowing that I don't need to always understand and I don't have to hold on to find justice. I don't need to shrink myself in order to live. I don't need to be afraid of what they might do. I gave myself permission to feel, to try and ultimately, to be. And it turns out, I like me. Once I stopped running, I found out that the giant wasn't as big as I'd made him out to be. When I stopped fighting myself, I found myself tapping in to a power that was undeniable and stronger than anything I'd ever found.

Seeking therapeutic help was a big step for me as a teenager. Growing up, a therapist was never something that was talked about or brought up despite me having multiple struggles that would have benefited from having someone to safely talk with. But of course, you can't have a child who's being sexually abused go see a therapist to address the issues unless you're okay with them talking about the sexual abuse. So, my parents made grand gestures with a few doctor's appointments. There were specialized appointments to scan my stomach for why I had such bad stomach pains all the time. I went to doctors' appointments to try to rule out anything wrong with my head to identify the causes of the migraines that plagued me. A high dose pharmaceutical regimen was finally prescribed to manage the symptoms as well as a restriction of foods that could be the migraine triggers (caffeine, chocolate, cheddar cheese). A laxative drink was given to encourage better bowel movements to perhaps reduce the stomach/intestinal pains. No doctor brought up the mental or emotional influences that might be causing the pains. No one ever suggested to me that my physical symptoms might be alleviated by addressing the underlying issues…the fear, the anxiety, the depression, the apathy. I didn't even know what anxiety was until I was a teenager and it wasn't until I was around 30 before I learned that migraines are related to anxiety and emotions, stored traumas and repressed pain.

If I brought up emotional issues beyond anxiety with a health care provider, it was met with a blank nod and smile, as if to brush it away. They agreed that low blood sugar, dehydration, lack of sleep, anxiety and hormones are all things that contribute to migraines. They praised me for being aware of that. They always turned to medications as the solution and when I turned down prescription painkillers, they almost pushed me aside. By that point, I was determined to not become a life-long customer of big Pharma. I know what one prescription leads to…another prescription. Higher doses, more side-effects and simply a masking of the symptoms was not my goal. What I sought was healing of the deep-seated causes that dwell deep within. No one seemed like they wanted to help me with that though. They seemed to just want to cover it up with a quick fix.

Where do migraines originate from? It depends who you ask. Most health-care providers, upon ruling out big things like a brain tumour etc., got me to make a migraine log or diary where I tracked and monitored what I ate each day, what and how much I drank, sleep, exercise and routine as well as rate migraines as they occur. What I was never told to include in said diaries was my emotional health and well-being in relation to the migraines. I must assume that many health care providers don't know that emotions and past traumas can directly play a role in migraines because with their motto of "do no harm", they would be doing harm to withhold that information from their patients. Stress causes migraines, this I was told. Yet no one offered any real solutions as to how to actually deal with the underlying causes of this "stress". I was given "coping mechanisms" read "ways to better deal with the stress that reduced migraine symptoms". The check-box could then be ticked off and I'd be sent on my way. No one addressed the elephant in the room. There seems to be a disconnection between the medical doctors and the psychiatrist. If the medical doctor suspects someone needs more help, then off to the psychiatrist. But that is when the physical symptoms have been addressed.

When I was sent to the psychiatrist, it was one pill then another. Before I knew it, I was on several medications and still feeling pretty horrible. No matter what medication I tried that they prescribed, the anxiety and depression still remained. The psychiatrists' solutions were always another pill or a higher dosage. It was me deciding that I was done with this way that caused the biggest change in my mental health. I quit all the medications, cold-turkey. All of them. Was it easy? No. There were a lot of withdrawal symptoms. I had extreme mood swings, more panic attacks and was flooded with emotions and compelling thoughts. I was determined though. It wasn't long before the withdrawal symptoms decreased and the fog, as well as the side-effects, from the prescriptions went away. For the first time in the longest time, I actually was able to connect with myself. The anti-depressants and anti-anxiety medications did nothing to help me. It was the hard inner work that brought true freedom and healing from the debilitating anxiety and depression. I wasn't as well-informed about herbal medicines at that time and I would definitely have used herbal aids through the withdrawal process as well as the healing journey if I had been.

I can only imagine how revolutionary it would be if trauma was actually addressed by the medical system. If health care providers were actually trained in true, holistic, deep trauma healing, I believe most illnesses would practically disappear. Herbs, holistic remedies, detoxing and fasting would likely clean up the remnants that remained. Have you ever felt like you were just a number? Have you ever wondered why the doctor seemed to care more about getting you in and out of the office than he did about your true well-being? I don't know that we can really blame them—medical doctors are among the most heavily indoctrinated. It's just sickening to me though how much they profit off of us being sick. If you really look at it, how can they actually treat patients from an unbiased standpoint when they stand to profit (or lose their profits) off of us based on how they treat us? They don't make money if we are well. When you see how one-sided the whole system is, how they've thrown true science out of the window and subscribed to this big Pharma profit system, it's easy to see why the general populus is so ill. I look forward to the new way (read the old way) being implemented where herbs and holistic regimens based on the four principles of emotional, physical, mental and spiritual well-being are all equally considered and utilized when working with a patient.

The system/society teaches girls to be divided. The goody-two-shoes Christian girl looks down on the girl wearing the tight-fitting clothes and going to parties and calls her a whore while the party girl looks at the Christian girl and calls her frigid. All the while though, there's no difference. Each girl is being used and abused by the same system. One just might get used on the dance floor while the other one might take her turn in the church basement. As long as I think I'm different than you and you think you're different than me, the system wins. The system hates us and the way it perpetuates itself is through division and hate. Pick a side, it doesn't matter which; the system created them all. It's all a bunch of rules, a whole list of dos and don'ts. Erase the invisible lines and you'll see though that we are all the same. And if we all stand together, we take back the power that has always been ours. Good girl, bad girl, nice girl, mean girl, badass, bitch, princess, queen…it doesn't matter which label you pick; you're still stuck in the maze. They are just names. Names mean nothing unless you buy into the lie that they hold some meaning and let them do something to you.

We had the same necklaces, my mother and I. I mean not exactly the same, hers was a different colour and had a different word bead on it than mine, but they were otherwise the same. But I liked hers and one day, completely in an unordinary fashion, we somehow traded necklaces. We didn't share anything, ours was not that kind of a relationship, but for some reason we did that day. And then after a long time, or perhaps a few days, suddenly there she was in my room and she was near my dresser where I assumed the necklace was. She was over there asking for her necklace back. Lo and behold, there was her necklace, broken on the dresser. I had no idea how it got broken but she didn't believe me. She asked me who I thought had broken it then and I told her that perhaps it was the cat because maybe the cat climbed on the dresser and chewed it. I had no idea how it could be broken; I'd forgotten I'd even had her necklace. She didn't believe me though and was sure I'd broken it.

Another time, she looked at the head board of my bed. It was an oak headboard, quite fancy for this spacious queen bed they'd bought for me. She pointed and shrieked about something on the headboard. I had no idea what she was talking about so I looked. A piece of the wood was ripped up a bit from it and it was painted over now with a similar-colored paint as the color of the wood, as if to hide the broken headboard. Again, I had no idea one, how the headboard got damaged like that in the first place and then two, I didn't even know where I would have found paint that colour (or any paint for that matter) to have painted it with and three, I had no recollection of ever having painted it either. Yet, she didn't believe me. It didn't matter what I said, in her opinion, I was lying and now I'd have to earn back her trust. How could she trust me again if I broke her things and then tried to hide it? I agreed aloud with her that I would have to earn back her trust while internally knowing that I hadn't done anything. Yet, I felt as guilty as if I had.

They were these kinds of scenarios, this twisted, sick, psychological abuse that cut at a deep part of the soul, deeper than all the sexual abuse ever did. I'll say it again, as I've said it before, as horrible as the sexual abuse was, it was nothing compared to the long-lasting effects of the psychological abuse. That cold, calculated, sick messing with my mind; the way they'd get me to doubt my own words, actions, my very being. The way they'd come at me with mental boxing gloves on and beat me up around the ring there for awhile and then suddenly, they'd rip off the gloves and just giv'er. No matter how hard I tried (and oh, I really tried) to be prepared or try to at least somewhat anticipate it, I could never keep up. There was always some new rule or changing of an old rule. There was always something I must have misinterpreted or some unspoken something that made no sense yet I was expected to make sense of it and keep it all together. And if I had the audacity to "fall apart", then that was my mess to clean up and my price to pay too. The path to healing from the psychological mess I was after that kind of abuse was nothing short of an arduous journey and yet it was as simple as unhooking the cart from the horse.

  I spent a lot of time beating myself up for how long the healing was taking. I felt like I was doing that wrong too. Looking back though, I can see how much foundational work was done while on the outside it may have seemed that no changes were being made. I spent a lot of time soul-searching, researching healing modalities and practices, learning about meditation and mantras, trying to implement said practices, listening to healing music and reading the writings of influential trauma and wellness healers. During this time, I started rewiring my brain after all of the negative pathways had been formed. And when I was finally ready, it was like flipping on a switch; the lights just sort of came on. Sure, there were a few kinks to work out but my overall message to you is to trust your own inner healer. You know exactly what you need to do to heal. Don't let anyone tell you that you're doing it wrong. Only you know what you must do…and only you can do it.

Chapter 9

Terrified

The day they took me to the ward to see the psychiatrist was a big day. I was referred to him after the pediatrician saw that I was too underweight and I wasn't able to see that I was. Before she referred me though, she made my mother leave the room and talked to me privately. She wanted to know if I was doing drugs, smoking, having sex or if I was being abused. I was adamant that none of those things applied to me. I restated that I was fat and just needed to lose some more weight. I weighed just over 100 lbs and wasn't much more than skin and bones. My back was covered in bruises from my spine protruding from my skin. My hair was thin and falling out. I was freezing cold all the time. I couldn't focus and the straight A honors student was struggling to remember basic math.

I wish that I'd been able to clearly look at what had been happening to me, been able to tell her and get out of there. Instead, they got to look like the clueless and caring parents who just wanted the best for their daughter. They looked like they were so supportive pulling out all the stops and bringing me in for assessment, both of them, because they didn't want me to die. Now that is truly it though. They didn't want me to die. That was their reasoning. It wasn't because they truly cared about my emotional distress or the psychological reasons that I might be struggling like this. No, they wanted their image preserved and they used guilt and shame, coercion and manipulation of a sick and abused child to get what they wanted. The psychiatrist made me get weighed and I felt so embarrassed to do so in front of my father that he stepped out, again looking like such a kind and considerate man. The verdict, an eating disorder, most certainly. Anorexia. Classic anorexia--refusing to eat, fear of food and being fat, excessive exercise. The psychiatrist informed them that I showed signs of being willing to improve as an out-patient so was given a chance to try that before moving to in-patient. My mother, ever the supportive one, later threatened me that if I didn't improve quickly, she would drag me in to the in-patient ward and then, everyone would know about this shameful thing I was doing to myself.

And there I would go again, a deer in the headlights. I would be worried that he was going to be mad again. I was scared that he would yell and that I wouldn't know what to do. I would feel put on the spot. I felt like I was standing there naked and everyone was staring at me. My heart would start to pound and I would feel this pit in my stomach. I couldn't really think anymore and I felt like I'd done everything wrong and maybe I should die because all I did was hurt everyone and make things harder. I felt like I caused more heartache than joy. Yet I still knew deep inside that I hadn't done it all that way and those were lies once again. It was like the necklace all over again. They twisted and manipulated the truth until I was so confused that I didn't even know what was up anymore. I knew that breaking the necklace and hiding it would have been wrong to do and I couldn't remember ever doing that yet I felt this guilt inside me like I had done that, that somehow it really was my fault that it was broken. It was no different when my husband started going off on me. I'd freeze because I carried so much shame and guilt inside that I resonated with what he was saying on some deep level.

At the same time, I'd know that it was skewed, bubbling up from his unhealed traumas as well as my own. Yet, it was so hard to sift through in the heat of the moment. I'd feel like I was stuck in that same thing as my whole life, over and over again…damned if I did, damned if I didn't.

Over and over, we would repeat the same wretched dance with small differences until eventually, we truly looked at each other and said no more. We each chose to make a different choice, a better choice. And together, we started holding each other accountable for our actions and inactions. The more traumas we unearthed and subsequently let go of, the closer we got and the deeper our relationship grew. Looking back, it was when I was able to adopt an attitude of unattachment that I was able to let go of the pain that used to haunt me. It was my attachment that kept me shackled to my abusers and those cycles of abuse.

When did they take it away? Or better, when did I get tricked or worn down enough to give up? Was it when I was engrossed reading my special book about castles? I would lie on my tummy on my bed and be so involved in the book, transported to a magical land of noble knights and fair ladies, that I wouldn't hear the door opening until I felt her hand between my legs. Or I'd be sitting on the ground reading the book and then my hair would be grabbed. I'd be yanked to my feet and thrown face down on the bed, my pants ripped off and a cock (or something like it) shoved in me. Just a beautiful book and I would be so involved with it that I didn't notice the door opening until they were there doing the dirty things they did. So yeah, I may not remember exactly when I gave up but I do understand why.

I never knew when it was coming next or why or how or from whom. There was no mercy, no rest for the weary, no consideration for the hurting. There was just a desire and people with no self-control.

I started splitting off parts of myself because it was too much to understand. Something that felt so good sometimes was also so very wrong. What was so embarrassing was also so much fun. What was fun sometimes often turned terrifying and painful quickly with no warning. They told me to feel ashamed of all parts of me. They instructed me to hide all of myself away and pretend that it didn't exist. You might be wondering why I didn't just say no or how could I have possibly not known that it wasn't right. Perhaps you wonder why I didn't tell a Sunday School teacher, one of my friend's parents, the librarian, someone, anyone?

It didn't matter who I knew, they all did it too. And if I did tell, then sometimes it turned into two--the one whom I told to and the one I told on. And let me tell you, the lesson they tried to teach about keeping your mouth shut was really not very fun. But why not say no? Sure, try it and then see how it feels to be stripped naked, blindfolded, gagged, tied up and hung upside down, alone in a closet for however long until you're freezing and shaking and the restraints are hurting. Listen to them come in and then feel them cum in. And there's absolutely nothing you can do. A janitor's closet has lots of items that work well for sexually torturing a child. Being locked alone in that dark closet in the far corner of the church where no one could hear my muffled cries for help or where no one came in response to my cries for help, was perhaps one of the darkest experiences of my childhood.

I spent a lot of time being afraid of the closet without allowing myself to actually look at the closet. I've said it was a lot of different things over the years that I was scared of and maybe I was scared too of those things. But let me tell you something, there's just something about that closet and the terror that was provoked in me there. It was a place where you could easily question if God even exists. It may have been in a church but they desecrated one of God's holy temples there. So, it was pretty for sure after that that I didn't question it when they told me it was my turn to go to the special room.

And I played my part as well as I could. I took all my clothes off the way they told me to; I danced and moved my body around the room the way they liked. I went over to the men who summoned me from around the circle and I stood there waiting for them to finish. I let them finish however they wanted and made sure they were happily satisfied. I washed my face in the bathroom before going back out to complete my performance. I learned to have fun while performing. I did have fun performing. They gave me a part, told me how to play that part and then I tried my darnedest to get the gold star.

The closet. I remember being put in the closet, more than once. I remember one time walking in church when I was maybe 7-9 years old and suddenly this person grabs me and puts me in the closet. I remember them putting me in the closet when I didn't behave or at least that's why I thought they were doing it though I'm not sure what I did wrong. They would put me in this closet. I think it was dark or they blindfolded me. Either way, I couldn't see. They took off all my clothes and they tied me upside down somehow. And they'd leave me there. Alone. With the spiders. So many spiders. I felt like they were crawling all over me, in me, up me, everywhere. And there was nothing I could do. I'd scream and I'd cry. I'd try to get loose and I'd pee and poop myself. And no one cared. I couldn't breathe because of the fear or maybe the pressure of being tied upside down. My head would pound from the pressure and I felt like I might explode. My hands and feet would go numb and I'd be so very, very cold. People (or things) would come and go from the closet. I didn't always know that they were there and sometimes I could hear them. And they would do things to me. Terrible, painful things. They would hit me. They would pour liquids on me. They would smack me and whip me. They would poke me and stroke me. They would touch all over me. They would touch and hit me with things and they would put things in me. They would rape and assault me over and over until they were done or it was someone else's turn.

Sometimes it was gentle and sometimes it was very, very painful. They would put things inside me that hurt so badly I thought I was breaking. There would be stuff all over me and in me--in my mouth and my eyes and my nose and my pee-pee and bum. I'd scream and no one cared. I'd scream and they would care and they'd gag me. They'd put spiders on me or at least that's what they said. They'd leave me alone in there with the spiders, at least that's also what they said. And in that closet, I wondered if God really existed. I would enter a realm, a place within myself where I questioned what reality even was. What kind of a planet is this where people and creatures do these things to others, to children? The closet was a place where I learned that for some, there seem to be no rules and they can do whatever they like, without consequence. It was a place of such abject horror and apathy that I would have been willing to do almost any of the depraved sexual acts they wanted me to perform so as to not have to be put back in the closet.

Creatures. I remember some of the creatures. Weird shapes, etheric beings that seemed to defy the rules of this world. They would come and go and do things that made no sense such as appear out of nowhere or go from small to large. The worst was her, my grandmother. In real life, she was this fat, loud, over-bearing, old lady. And when she transformed into her other shape, she was not just a woman. She was part spider, part human. Her upper body was human and her lower body was spider. And she was giant or so it seemed to me, a small child. She would suddenly be there, in her evil spider shape and she would terrify me. She would wrap me in her web until I couldn't move. She would lock me there, naked, covered in her sticky web while she watched me struggle there. Laughing, she would record it all as she paralyzed me in that shameful state. And I'd be stuck there, splayed open. She'd scurry over there, with her recording equipment all around, and she would stick her long spider legs inside me, over and over again. She'd run those hairy, creepy legs over my open pee-pee and it was so shameful having this disgusting woman-spider make me squirm and that amazing feeling would happen too. And then she would plunge her legs inside me and they'd go so far up inside me that my eyes felt like they would pop out of my head as I screamed trying to get away.

She'd turn around and place her spider parts on my face so all I could do was be there, suffocated by her as she shoved her legs inside me. She would put these sucking things on my pee-pee and pull them off, over and over. Leeches maybe. She would show me how huge she had made my pee-pee become, so grotesquely huge. And she'd record how hideous I looked. She would touch it with her spider legs and with her hands. She would slap it and she would hit it. She would put her face on it and bite it, lick it, suck it, eat it. I would feel immense pleasure and horrible pain. And all the while feeling so terribly mortified as if my face was literally burning with shame.

She would come up beside me and stroke my face, as if to comfort me, as she performed her sadistic, satanic torture on the rest of my body, particularly my pee-pee. And I would convulse there, bouncing on her web. It was like some sick, twisted carnival ride that just never seemed to stop. And the world would spin in great spirals around me as I was held in this place of seemingly timeless eternity. And sometimes, I could see my mother and other family members above me, as if I was under the floor beneath them. I could see them and faintly hear them but they couldn't see or hear me...or at least they pretended that they couldn't. And I was trapped there with her, with no one to save me. I could see them there. I'd scream for them to save me but nobody could hear me, nobody came. So maybe that explains to you a bit of why I had such an abject fear of spiders. The kind I knew of could do unheard of and unspeakable things. Perhaps she was dressed up in a costume. Perhaps I was so traumatized by the terror of what she did and said that the woman-spider descriptor was the best to fit what I couldn't comprehend. Or maybe she really did change form into what I described above. What is clear though is that my grandmother did sadistic, torturous, terrifying and abusive things to me, over and over again, while I screamed, cried and begged for her to stop.

~

"Good, Little Christian Girl"

Good, little Christian girl who does exactly what she's asked.

She reads her Bible, prays, follows all the rules, tries so hard to keep everyone happy.

She's the first one to volunteer, first one with her arm up ready with an answer, knows the verses by heart, arms up in the air singing her heart out.

Oh, Good, Little Christian Girl, can they see what you really are under there?

No one seems to notice when her smile starts getting fake.

No one seems to notice when she starts to have less to say.

No one seems to notice when the enthusiasm isn't really there.

No one seems to care when her clothes start getting baggier or notice when she starts to lose her hair.

No one seems to notice when she stops leading prayer.

When they kick her off the worship team, no one really bats an eye.

No one's there to support her when she feels cast aside.

No one takes a second look when she quickly pulls her sleeves down or seems to wear a sweater or long-sleeves all the year long.

They think she just wants to help out when she's too busy to sit down and eat.

No one seems to see her wipe the hidden tear on the sheet.

To her, the future seems so bleak and they are all so content with her being so meek.

No one follows up with her after she comes forward to report the creepy Sunday School teacher and the lonely hallway.

Were they just happy that all she seemed to remember was that she felt uncomfortable and was worried that the seclusion in that area might harm another girl?

When the weight piled on, they didn't have anything then to say either.

But when it fell off again, they praised her even higher.

When she signed up to help at each event around, there was gratefulness, yes, but no real care for her to be found.

No arms around to support her when her world gave way, no hand to hold hers when she couldn't see the way.

Unless she did everything they wanted, they couldn't care less and when she stopped walking through that doorway, she wasn't even missed.

"Oh, just another one who's gone the Liberal way. University has changed her like so many others these days."

She can't say quite why but she knows the fires rage hotter when she's there and it's better to not have them near.

She can't hold it together when she's there anymore so she leaves there to walk through another church door.

This one's really no different or maybe it is but she's been abused for so long that it's hard to think clear.

Every church wall seems the same and the pews are just ew.

She wishes that someone would really see her and take away all her fear.

~

It was that feeling, that groggy feeling, that unclear feeling. It was hard to keep it together when that feeling came in. It got so overwhelming. The feeling grew and grew. I don't know what shook it. Sometimes it was just doing something else but mostly time was what would fix it; I had to wait for the feeling to pass. The triggers were countless so how to let go of them all I didn't know. I don't remember when exactly the feeling came to be. I remember it first when I was small, asleep I think, in my room. I remember waking up on my back in my bed with my legs up in the air and my parents both there as I was screaming and my legs hurt so badly. And I saw over in the air these eyes, these spirals going around and around and I was all loopy, groggy and totally without a clue. When I later asked them about it, they just said I'd been sick. As a child, I simply accepted what they had to say. But I remember them now, holding me down. I remember them poking and prodding. I remember them smelling funny with their glasses of red liquid. They clinked their glasses as they laughed and fell half over on each other. I didn't really understand what they were doing. Why were they in my room? Why were they lifting up my sheets? Why were they pulling off my panties? They took turns holding my legs apart just like they took turns doing something to me down there on my pee-pee. I was so tired and I felt so funny. At one point, one of them was sitting behind me, holding me and holding my legs with their legs. It hurt my legs and they gave me some of their bad juice. He was staring at my pee-pee like he was a doctor or something. I was so confused and so out of it. And they kept laughing and clinking their glasses. I just wanted to go back to sleep. I guess eventually it got rough because I was screaming and my legs and pee-pee hurt so badly.

There was a period of time when I was around 19 when some of the medications I were on were switched because I wasn't getting any relief from the depression and anxiety I was experiencing. I had an adverse reaction to the

medication the psychiatrist prescribed to me and it flipped
a switch inside of me. I couldn't sleep for days. I would sit
vibrating on a chair, unable to hold still. The hunger I'd
suppressed for years was unleashed like a savage beast and
I couldn't stop myself from consuming everything I could.
I think I blew over $1000 on food in a couple months—this
was just extra food for me to binge on. I already ate
everything in sight at home. I'd bake batches of cookies and
freeze them in bags for the family. Then later be unable to
stop myself and I'd go out to the garage freezer, grab the
bag and hide on the garage steps where I then would
proceed to eat the entire bag. I'd eat frozen loaves of bread,
gallons of ice-cream, pastries and biscuits. I was so
embarrassed but I couldn't stop myself from shoving my
face full of food. All I thought about was food. I felt like I
was starving and there was nothing that could fully satisfy
my hunger. I'd be stuffed full but still felt starving and
would just keep eating.

To describe the helplessness I felt at this point is
difficult. After having prided myself for having such a great
ability to control my food consumption, this was a major
blow to my ego. I couldn't stop the numbers from climbing
on the scale. I had to buy clothes bigger than I'd ever bought
before in my life. The psychiatrist actually sent me to her
eating disorders group therapy at that time. Imagine the
looks on the anorexic girls' faces when I, now a bit lumpy,

was sitting in the group where they were talking about being triggered at Easter by their parents eating Easter candy in front of them. If I didn't eat, I couldn't sleep at all. It was as simple as that. And when I binged, it didn't necessarily mean I could actually sleep because sometimes I still couldn't and it also didn't stop the nightmares. It just helped take the edge off, I guess, and I really had no control over it. The binging also went hand-in-hand with the self-harm. I felt disgusting because I was eating so much and couldn't stop. I couldn't come back into my body. I was always feeling fuzzy, numb and out of it. It was this hollow, empty, soul-sucking feeling with a vein of terror running through it and this inability to turn off. And just like I couldn't stop myself from eating, I couldn't stop myself from turning to the knife. There was something about the sharp pain that took the edge off of how I was feeling and somehow made me feel like I was still going to survive. It made me feel like I was still alive instead of stuck inside of this body, trapped and helpless. The psychiatrist took me off the medication but it took months before things started to get back to "normal".

Chapter 10

The Call of That Little Girl

When I was diagnosed with an eating disorder at 14, the psychiatrist was all business. Prescriptions and routine tests were just some ticks on his normal checklist. He passed me off to a dietician set up a meal plan. The plan was that I would be given a few months to show improvement on gaining weight/eating as well as obviously not losing any more weight and then I would be allowed to stay as an outpatient. On the way home, my mother who'd acted so sweet and caring at the appointment turned back into her usual self. She threatened me that if I did not start eating, she would drag me kicking and screaming to go live on the ward and then everyone would know that I had this shameful problem. She coerced and manipulated me into starting on the medication the doctor prescribed then after her threat of being hospitalized and everyone knowing. That and driving me to my appointments was the extent of her support. There was no checking in to see how I was doing emotionally. There was no counseling to address the reason behind developing the eating disorder or why I was coping this way. Actually, she found it so triggering sitting in the waiting room at the ward because of staring at all those "sick girls" (as if I wasn't sick too) that I just finally told her to wait in the car. Eventually, I just drove myself.

The psychiatrist was a joke…he himself probably had several mental health disorders and he popped his pills freely in front of me during our appointments. He talked more about his plants than my concerns and thought his joke name he had for me was just so funny. When he found out that I was self-harming, he simply asked if I'd used duct tape to hold together any of the wounds because that's what he'd heard some other patients had done. I finally got a referral by my own request to a psychologist who specialized in eating disorders because I felt so alone and unsupported. I often wished that I could just stay on the ward. It seemed much more peaceful, safer and supportive there. I felt like it was this quiet womb to be warm and protected in. But I didn't want to be forced to have a feeding tube stuck down my nose nor required to stay there so I did everything in my power to stay well enough that I wouldn't be hospitalized. I also was so ashamed of having an eating disorder so being hospitalized would have been so shameful as then I was sure everyone would know what a screw-up I was.

At first, I followed the dietician's plan with great care and interest. For the first time in my life, I learned about things like the food pyramid and nutrition. I became overly obsessed with food and while this dietician did not believe in counting calories, instead opting to utilize color-coded "meal cards" as a way of getting away from counting calories, I found it quite hilarious. Did she really think I was that stupid that I then wouldn't count the calories in my head? Each card was still worth either 50, 100 or 200 calories depending on what it was. Anyhow though, I took home the given cards and obediently utilized them to gain the required weight. Every time she weighed me and I gained weight, she applauded and I felt like I died a little bit inside. She told me to note the point at which my periods came back as that would mark an important threshold number.

When my periods did come back, I was dismayed that she then told me I needed to gain another 10-15 pounds. She explained that I could easily lose 5 pounds if I got sick and then that would risk the periods and a 10-15 pound buffer zone was a good way to protect my overall well-being. Eventually though, I did reach a healthy weight and as time went on, everything seemed fine on the outside.

I was doing well in school, weighed a healthy weight, was getting ready for university and to graduate etc. etc. During grade 12, I ended up with a couple spares. Some might have utilized this time for studying but I used the one at the end of the day for getting more hours at a job so I could afford to go to university. The morning spare proved to be a great time for that healing anorexic to start going to the gym. It started out innocently enough but it wasn't long until it became an obsession again.

I wasn't okay unless I pushed myself to the max for the entire spare. I started running on the treadmill because it was the fastest way to burn calories. Up and down the hills, as fast as I could go. Then I turned to interval training to burn as much fat as possible. I became overly familiar with the weight machines to make my shoulders and arms bigger and my fatty legs smaller and more muscular. When that wasn't enough, I took to also running outside after school or on lunches or both. I was obsessed with exercise and became a fanatic. Now that I have a healthy, balanced relationship with exercise, those hours spent learning about exercise and nutrition have been instrumental in aiding me in helping myself and others. At the time though, it was a sick and unhealthy obsession that arose out of a desire to get away from those feelings of shame, dirtiness, grossness, confusion and self-hatred.

By the time my parents realized how much weight I had lost the first time, I was pretty far gone. I think it became pretty apparent to them (and to me) that something was wrong when I was taken to the exam room for a math exam and I blanked. I couldn't even remember how to use the calculator and this was coming from the straight A honors student! At that point, I was just sure something was wrong with me. I couldn't sleep then either; my stomach hurt from not eating but I was certain that I was fat. I kept yelling at myself in my head for feeling hungry still when I'd already eating some frozen beans!

I'd put my headphones in my ears to drown out the voices in my head so I could fall asleep at night. I was so sure everyone hated me and that I had done so much bad. I remember lying on the floor on the stairs at home just hysterically laughing then bawling my eyes out while my family just stared wide-eyed at such a crazy display of emotion. I was in my room on my bed once crying with my mother and my brother or brothers came in, wondering what I was crying about. And I went on and on about how I was such a bad person and how sorry I was. And my brother just looked at me incredulously as if to say what are you talking about, you never even get in trouble for anything because you don't ever do anything wrong, how can you feel like this? And I knew this was true on the surface but somewhere deep inside, it didn't resonate. I felt, deep down, that I was this dirty, bad person who was going to go to hell and I was running as hard and fast as I could to stop that demon from wrapping his hand around my neck and taking me.

I wonder if my family really thought that increasing calories, stopping exercise, returning to a healthy weight and taking some medication would actually resolve the eating disorder. I wonder what ED recovery would have looked like with a supportive family that truly wanted to understand where I was coming from and cared less about their image and more so, weren't selfishly motivated to ensure that their little sex doll was still around to fulfill their needs. How would one be able to care about their child's emotional needs if the very things they were doing to them were of course harming them emotionally? Further, would they have even been aware of what my emotional needs were? Or would they have been so ignorant and blinded by their own desires that they couldn't see anything else?

Is just the fact that they were doing what they were doing in and of itself not completely suggestive that they were emotionally immature at best or more likely, that they were adults coping with the emotional damage and abuse of their own deranged childhoods in the best way they knew how? I make no excuses for their behaviour. Adults are responsible for their own choices and behaviors. And what they did was wrong. I simply wish to explore that it is not as simple as saying they had needs and desires and chose to use me to fulfill them. On the one level, it is that simple. Going further though, one can begin to see the way the sick culture we have been raised in fosters, even cultivates, this sort of deranged behaviour. Society has cultivated an environment that emasculates males, objectifies women, promotes a self-entitled feminist agenda then erases the genders, all the while placing people in a life-sucking, no-win situation where the only goal the system has is to divide so the system can win. And that's not even going into the sick, terrifying, demoralizing Satanic and other kinds of abuse that are occurring all over the world.

I want you to understand something. What happened to you as a child is not your fault. No child is ever to blame for any of the actions an adult took. I can hear the questions in your head because I heard them in mine. But I seduced him! I told them I wanted to. I liked it so much. It really was a fun game! I asked to play. I could've told someone and I didn't. On and on. The truth though is this—it doesn't matter if you took all your clothes off, climbed on top of your parent and had sex with them while they slept. That would still have not been your fault. I can hear you saying, asking how? They weren't even awake. Correct, they weren't but no child would ever do that unless they had been trained (read, abused) to do so. A child's only job is to be a kid. To grow and learn and play. No child should have to wonder if their smile is big enough to please their audience's sexual desires nor should they have to watch their legs while they are being railed to see if they might need to lose some more weight because their legs jiggle while their dad rapes them.

I want you to know that it's okay if you don't remember very much of it. That's a normal trauma response. Your body did exactly what it needed to do to protect itself. When the trauma that you were undergoing was too much for you to handle, your body loved you so much that it did exactly what it needed to do to keep you safe in the only way it knew how--through the built-in self-protective mechanisms embedded deep within your code. How were you supposed to handle it day in and day out, night after night? I know how exhausting it was wondering which way or from whom it was going to cum (I mean, come) next. For me, everything was sexual. It either started, ended or was interrupted because of sex. I'd get in trouble and I'd be on my knees. I'd get it right and I'd be up on the table.

I'd make a mistake and I'd be bent over the table or strung up in the closet. I'd be reading a book and then I'd be down on the ground. I'd be in the washroom and suddenly, I wasn't alone. It felt like it was too much to bear sometimes and I too forgot. Yet it started to creep back in. In the still moments when I couldn't keep going anymore, flashes of the past would flitter across my mind. Sounds, smells, sights and sensations jarred buried pieces of the past into my present in a wild cacophony of experience. Sometimes I pushed the memories away because I wasn't ready and I didn't want to see it. But eventually, the call of that little girl deep inside me was too loud for me to ignore. She beckoned me deeper and I decided to stop running. Once I made that conscious choice, the past began to emerge from the dark recesses where I had buried it.

There were two voices inside my head. Some call them two wolves, the white wolf and the black wolf, the good wolf and the bad wolf. Some say it's the ego and the higher self. At the end of the day, no matter which way you label them, I believe it's just you. You are the one yelling at you. You are the one praising you. You are your worst critic and also your best friend. You know yourself better than anyone else and you also don't know yourself at all. You love yourself yet you also hate yourself. You're the one who hurts you, no one else can. Wait, you say, that's not true. So and so did this to me and so and so did that. Those were very hurtful things, abusive even. They traumatized me! If they hadn't done those things, I'd be a completely different person today. It's because he raped me that I hate men. It's because she told me I was fat that I have an eating disorder. I have anxiety because of an enflamed family environment. I don't know how to sit still because when I sat still, someone always came over and took it away. I hear all your reasons, I really do. And I get why you're saying them. They make sense even. They've been words I've said before too.

And they really are just words created by an empty culture to further divide. As long as there is an abuser, there has to be a victim. And as long as you are attached to the victim card, it is very hard to rise and stand in your own power. Remembering yourself as a child dancing provocatively on a table or unabashedly displaying your beauty for everyone to see exactly how they groomed you to is not a reason to now pack your bags, book a one-way ticket to another country and change your name. What they did was wrong. Period. But as long as we are attaching labels like shame and victim to it, it is very hard to let go of. With an attitude of unattachment, we are able to observe what happened, truly heal and transmute. And from that place, we can speak the truth and rise into our power. They've indoctrinated us through the all the systems to hold this shame deep within ourselves. And we all feel it. It doesn't matter if you're the church pastor or the alcoholic, the CEO or the high-school drop-out—everyone, unless they've embarked on the healing journey, is operating from this low-level of shame. Some of us are really good at hiding it. But if you look closely, I bet you'll soon be able to see the ones who hold the most shame. They are not just your over-achievers, the perfectionists and the workaholics. You might even find it's people you know...it might even be you.

I never realized how much shame I held inside. I didn't see how much of what I did was based off of shame or a desire to feel less ashamed. For a long time, I refused to truly take a good look at the shame because I felt too ashamed. I was too proud also to admit how ashamed I felt. I told myself things like: I'm a good person; there's no shame here. I try so hard to do everything right, I'm only a little ashamed when I do something wrong. And that's a good thing, it motivates me to do better, to try harder! Fair enough but at what point does the shame cease to be a great motivator and instead starts to be a soul-sucking, thief of life? At what point does it stop? For me, it started to bleed out everywhere.

Where I once yelled at myself for burning some food and then utilized that shame to make a better meal the next time, eventually I stopped saying anything nice to myself at all. I ripped myself a new one because I burnt a piece of toast for breakfast for the kids, then I beat myself up when I forgot to put an apple in with my husband's work lunch I'd made. Then I'd verbally smack myself up the head because I'd go to get the kids dressed for the day and see that I'd forgotten to put the load of laundry on. Next, I'd call myself a few names when I went to wash the breakfast dishes because I hadn't gotten all the supper dishes cleaned up. Then I'd replay the argument my husband and I'd had the other day and repeat everything he said bad about me that I could remember over and over in my head. On and on it would go until everything got darker and darker and life seemed pretty bleak.

Sometimes I look back and watch my past self beating me up for each and every thing. I yelled at myself for taking a nap two days after giving birth. I have beaten myself up for not washing the dishes when I've had a migraine so bad that I was throwing up and couldn't sleep for two days. I've told myself that I'm not worth anything because I couldn't seem to release the trauma completely and found myself repeating the same old self-destructive patterns over and over. It wasn't until I committed to doing things differently that I saw real change. When I finally took accountability and became responsible for all of myself, healing was able to slide in. You see, as long as you choose to find someone to blame for how you feel inside, for the way you talk to yourself, for the state of your life, you give all your power away. You play the victim.

And a victim doesn't end the cycle of abuse. Just like the abuser, the victim mentality helps perpetuate the cycle of abuse. When you claim back your power, it doesn't matter if they call you names or spread their hate because no one can truly beat you down anymore. No one can take your words away, your truth. And when they don't get anything from you anymore, well, what's the point for them anyhow? So, in stepping out of the victim mentality, the self-blame and shame just sort of fall away. If that negative self-talk truly no longer holds any power, unconditional love and positive mantras can instead begin to take hold and rewrite the pathways of old.

Chapter 11

Stifling My Voice

Why wasn't I standing up for myself? Why was I struggling to use my voice? It all goes back to the closet. Standing up for myself equated to ending up back in the closet. Using my voice meant going back in the closet where they then gagged me and took my voice away. But I was the only one who gagged myself as an adult! Who was throwing me in the closet now? No one! And while I could see that, I was still so often helpless to change it. Deep inside of me was this relentless fear of the closet, of the punishment for standing tall, taking up space, choosing to try or speaking my truth. I was trained, and I further trained myself, to put my needs so far down there at the bottom that I didn't even know what they were anymore. The rationale? If I don't have any needs, then I can't get disappointed if my needs aren't met.

But hey, guess what? No matter how hard I pretended that I didn't have any needs, it still turned out that I did. It just came out in some pretty ass-backwards ways. Such as, I'd feel jealousy towards my kid for getting attention from my husband and if I even paid it any attention at all, I'd chalk it up to my inner child yelling because she didn't get that kind of attention from her father, that kind of wholesome, safe love that didn't end in repayment via sexual favors. And while that may be true on some level, it was also because I was mad at myself for not using my words to ask for what I wanted and needed. I let my shame and pride get in the way and there I stood out in the cold, crying like a victim that no one cared about me. I then cloaked myself in that gray cloak of shame and loneliness, wrapped it tightly around me so no one could get in and then wondered why I was standing there by myself crying with no one seeming to care!

And it all circled back to shame, to that deeply rooted core belief. It was also about the motivation. Somewhere deep inside, I didn't think I'd be motivated to do a good job if there was not some shame or fear of getting in trouble that was driving me. If I was making the meal out of love, would I really make it better? Perhaps, because at the very least there would be less resentment. I felt so disgusting at one point that even the thought of self-love made me feel like throwing up a bit inside. I was angry. Why were things the way they were? I was just over there, trying to do everything right and always feeling like I was doing everything wrong. Until I finally came to the realization that maybe I had been and maybe I hadn't been—and maybe that's the trick. As long as we are hung up on labels, on comparison and separation, we miss seeing the whole and the interconnectedness of it all. When we can step back and just breathe in the now, we can relax into true being where intuition leads and there is this perfect balance of the masculine and the feminine.

How to identify triggers when anything and everything seems to be a trigger? For me, the extent of the trauma and abuse was so great that I'm not sure I could identify all the triggers I accumulated over the years. From smells to sounds, to words to movements, they still can come in and hit me like a freight train, albeit not very often anymore. Sometimes I could see them and it would take a few minutes to let them go but other times it would have to recede. Other times, I had no idea that I'd even been triggered and I was gone. Or I could see that I was triggered and I was helpless to do anything other than slow down my going. I've used a variety of techniques such as those by Peter Levine and his somatic therapies that focus on creating safety in the body first before delving deep into the traumas, and these have been quite helpful in, at the very least, supporting me during those times.

But sometimes it just didn't feel like enough. I felt that it should already be healed up. I got it that they did those terrible awful things to me and I didn't want them too/didn't have a choice but why was I still being completely knocked flat on my back on the floor by the memories and triggers? I felt ashamed again that now I wasn't doing healing right. And over and over again it was the shame that I was clinging on to that kept me trapped in the prison I created for myself. It wasn't until I got sick and tired of carrying that weight around that I was able to make the most progress. It wasn't all at once. Rather it was bit by bit until it just came crumbling off pretty much altogether. Shame still tries to creep in sometimes but it doesn't take as long to see it for what it is. And instead of scolding myself for its appearance, I now have more of an open response to it. I ask it why it is here—what are you trying to show me? And with this attitude of openness, I've been able to go deeper into myself and truly embark on the journey of healing.

I held so much in. I wouldn't allow myself to speak or express angry words. I wouldn't defend myself or fight back. Maybe I did at one point but eventually I stopped; the risk to myself from the punishment that usually ensued just wasn't worth it or so I told myself. And all those feelings that I had that I lied to myself and said I didn't have, well I took them and I turned them on me. It wasn't safe for me to express them outwards so I expressed them inwards. I took my anger and I hurt myself. I starved myself. I cut myself. I became extremely depressed. I let others hurt me. I criticized and verbally abused myself worse than anyone else. I heaped punishments on myself for even existing. All those words I held back showed up in my jaw and other places in my body.

I ground my teeth so much over the years at night that I grounded one of my molars almost completely away. It broke off in pieces over a couple years and as it released major bits, it often was accompanied by a lot of pain. When I got my worst migraines, I'd rate them at a 10 for pain. Those are the ones where I'm throwing up from the pain. My mouth would sometimes get as bad as an 8. It was so hard to think with that pain. I kind of just wanted to check out and go read or maybe go to bed. I would lie in bed and just kind of ride the waves of the pain. It would peak and then it would relax, much like a contraction. When I was sitting up though, it was much worse and didn't really abate as much. After awhile, it also became really hard to open and shut my jaw on that side. From what I understand, the jaw and the pelvis are related and repression in either can be stored in the other. The sexual abuse combined with the stifling of my voice was a painful combination. I know I have shut my mouth over the years. I told myself that what I had to say was not important, that nobody cared. I was too scared to speak because of the consequences. Now I'm starting to have fear of what will happen if I don't speak.

When did I lose my self worth? Did I ever really have self-worth? I was never taught anything about self-worth growing up. Nobody mentioned self-esteem or believing in myself. I was just expected to follow the rules and do well in school, at church and at everything. No one ever talked about feelings. I didn't know what it meant to stand up for myself. Anything close to being about feelings was from church and things like the fruits of the Spirit. Somehow, I knew that I was supposed to grow these fruits and act that way. So, I would try and try to act that way. It was my goal to be loving and kind. I would pray and ask for help to be better. I was trained to perform and I based my self-worth on my performance…as well as their "ratings' of my performance. The sick part about performance self-worth is how based on outside validation it is and therefore how easily manipulated it can cause someone to become.

It is very easy to do things one would never normally do when they feel so desperately badly about themselves—they are willing to do almost anything to get that validation, that self-worth check that says that it is okay for them to be here, to breathe air even. I found myself slipping down a very slippery path. So long as they were praising me, it was almost a certainty that I would perform for my family. This pervasive thinking, this dependency on validation, this deficiency in self-worth really impacted my adult life. The very minimal boundaries I had with my husband soon became non-existent as I tried to shield myself because I was afraid. Running unchecked, my husband's childhood traumas and societal conditioning about women was a perfect storm for my childhood sexual and psychological abuse traumas as well as my dependency on performing and lack of boundaries. The first 6 years of our marriage were a very dark and tumultuous time in my life. I created a prison for myself that only I could break myself out of. Every pain, every shame, every rape, every scar...I chose to build them into walls around me, closing me in, locking me in behind what I thought was an impenetrable wall. But all it did was set me up to be abused over and over again. I believed them when they said it was my fault. All of them.

And when I totalled my car on our move across the country because of the pressure I was under and my husband lost it on me, screaming at me for the rest of the thousands of kilometers left in the trip or leaving me with his brother for the kilometres he couldn't handle being with me, I was at one of the lowest places of my adult life. I believed it was my fault and that I deserved him to be angry with me. The abuses I had experienced as a child conditioned me to accept that what he was doing was normal and what I deserved. I didn't know what a healthy relationship looked like. I didn't know what it was to be treated with respect or how to stand up for myself in a healthy way and demand respect. I would freeze into these trauma responses that were out of my control at that time and which would trigger him immensely. I would just stare at him, eyes glazed over, as his words would hit me like they were physical punches. I would freeze and I would dissociate as it became too much to handle. I was lost to that trauma response. My childhood traumas merged with my adult life and I was helpless to stop the continuing cycle of abuse. I was left feeling so apathetic because that life of safety I'd dreamed of having when I escaped my childhood family seemed to be out of reach.

And because I was terrified of what could happen, because I didn't believe in the power of my words, because I didn't believe that anyone would ever care to hear what I had to say, because I was beaten down and locked in the prison I'd created for myself, I was a perfect candidate for further abuse. It's not really too surprising what his family did to me. They knew what my husband was doing to me and they knew how much I wanted to protect my kids, how I'd do anything for them. So, when I was half-awakened to what felt like a cock in my vagina while we were staying over at my husband's brother's house, I just enjoyed it for a bit. It was from behind. And I just assumed it was my husband because who else would it be? But eventually I looked behind me (like I sometimes do, you know, to connect) and when I saw my husband's brother and his dad behind me, it felt like the floor was falling out beneath me, like I was crashing my car all over again. I didn't know what to do. I'm not even sure I was awake enough or not drugged enough to do anything.

I watched in horror as his father stared with this lunatic smile on his face as my brother-in-law raped me, with either his penis or some penis-like object. He was the only one close enough to me to be doing it but I couldn't see if it was his penis or something else. I was just stuck there, staring in shock. I wanted to cry; I wanted to scream but I could only stare there wordlessly watching as it felt like my whole world had just been ripped apart. I tried to move, I tried to do something, anything but I couldn't. This new family that I had had such high hopes for being a fresh start was just as messed up as the one I had left. I mean, it wasn't that surprising to me. Looking back, there were lots of signs and that feeling in my gut that I couldn't brush away but also couldn't logically explain. But to finally see the evidence there was both disheartening and hope-shattering and later, reassuring to know that my intuition had been spot on. I didn't tell anyone because I didn't think anyone would believe me, least of all my husband. And it was as simple (or as complicated depending on which way you want to look at it) as that. So, I shoved this assault deep inside myself to that place where I locked away all the other heinous abuses done to me. I tried even harder to please them all because I felt sure that it was only one wrong step and the lot of them would kick me to the door.

Always at the back of my mind the over-arching terror wondering who then would protect my kids from them? I remember my son breaking one of my in-law's cabinet doors. He was having a fit and kicked and it somehow broke the door. I lied to my mother-in-law and told her that I had tripped being pregnant and easily off-balance and broke it. She told me that it would probably be all right because they had the tools to fix it but I would need to tell my father-in-law myself as if to try and get me in trouble. I remember my mother-in-law coming over to quietly talk about the trouble I was in with my father-in-law (who was so upset with me but didn't want to risk causing a big scene with my crying she told me) because I had used the washer too late in the night and it had woken him up. All these subtle ways they would try to keep me subdued and in fear so that I would keep my mouth shut and do as they said. And I see how the abuses from my childhood, that deep-seated shame, that conditioning to accept abuse and be treated like crap set me up to be abused by my husband's family as well. The caveat though was that while I was unable to stand up for myself at that time, I was adamant that the kinds of sick abuses that were done to me wouldn't be done to my kids. So, I accepted abuses done to me (because I at that point wasn't able to see another way) in efforts to protect them until my husband was able to see enough to walk away.

My kids, husband and I were all really sick a year or two ago. I was just starting to get sick and I remember, we were all lying in bed, most everyone else a lot sicker. And I felt their presence and love surrounding me as it came in, the memory. I remembered being in the downstairs basement bedroom of my parent's home when I was a young adult and I don't remember much about what I was doing in there (it was my room as I was staying there at the time) but what I had been doing in there or what time of day etc., I don't remember. I just remember my youngest brother in there and he was really mad, he was pissed off, he was hurt, he was upset with me. And I felt that he was right, that he should be upset with me. I mean, I should have been there for him but I chose to not go. I chose to not go to his supper celebration for graduating because, well, something in me screamed that I shouldn't go and I didn't want to. And I was also sick. So, I didn't go. I had texted him that I wasn't going and I had felt the guilt as I told him no. So, when we were there in the bedroom, I felt ashamed and guilty for making my choice. I felt like a bad person, like a bad sister. And so, when he forced me onto the bed, when he pulled my pants down, when he held me down, when he raped me from behind…I don't know how much I tried to get away or really how hard I tried to stop him. I gave up.

I felt I deserved to be punished for my bad actions. I believed that I couldn't get away anyhow; he was bigger than me. When the memory came in, and now even still if I look at it again, I can hear myself screaming and sobbing that "I'm so sorry, I'm so sorry" over and over again. It hits down at a part of me right now even that gives me chills. I wonder how many times I screamed "I'm so sorry" and believed it was my fault and that I deserved to be punished, that I deserved whatever they did to me. I remember my head, turning it to the side on the bed and looking out towards the bedroom door. There, in the doorway shadows there, I saw my mother, just watching. And I can't help now but wonder if she didn't orchestrate it all. Was he even acting of his own accord? Or how many other times did he take it this far? It did flatten me for a bit though when I remembered.

I had really held that he was different, that he would never do something like that. I had so desperately wanted to believe that somehow, he just wasn't involved. I know, it's not really very realistic. I mean, everyone else was doing it to me but I just really wanted to believe that. I needed to believe that he was different somehow. He was the baby! He was our cute, little baby brother who we adored, who I adored. Now I can see how biased I was, how much I just didn't want to see what was there in front of me. But I get why I "forgot" and I'm proud of remembering when I did because I truly am trusting the process. The more I heal, the more I remember. And as I write, as I share, as I speak out, this pain finds a place to live outside of my body...and I feel the transmutation taking place. It's not linear, it's not perfect. But the trajectory is onward and upward.

It had been a pervasive, repetitive memory, less so as I've delved into the memory. But in the beginning, before I really began looking, she would call to me. I'd see her-- long, tangled, dirty brown-coloured hair wearing a stained, dirty, white dress all tattered and her mouth open in a soundless scream or sometimes a scream that I could hear. She'd be there with her tear-streaked face, white tracks through the dirt on her face. Her bare feet were scraped and bruised. Her body also battered and bruised. But she's called to me, she's announced she was there in the only way I guess that I would hear her. After I went on what some might call a "soul retrieval journey", she stood there, at the top of a grassy hill above a beautiful, peaceful meadow. She had her eyes closed, face tilted upwards basking in the warm sun streaming down on her face. I watched as she danced in the light. And I felt such peace and a wholeness that words cannot explain.

I realized that the medications I was taking as a teenager/young adult were not perhaps the meds I thought I was taking nor were they always the ones the doctor had prescribed. It is no wonder the doctor was so shocked that they weren't working but she just chalked it up to that I must need a higher dose. That happens sometimes. It is disturbing to think that they would go so far as to mess with my prescriptions for their own selfish gain. The amount I suffered, the immense pain I was in is something that sometimes brings shudders to me, even now. I can actually feel some of it now as then, well, there was so much that I was numb to. I walked around in a state of complete dissociation eventually; everything was too much. What had worked beautifully as a way to safeguard/protect myself from the horrendous sexual and psychological abuse became a way to escape anything that fractured the small semblance of peace I held. By separating myself from the actuality of my life, I in turn, eventually became somewhat separated from myself. The unconscious protective mechanisms of my child-brain would have been fine if the trauma was only once or even a couple of times and then I had been supported and nurtured into a state of healing and wholeness. This, as for many other abuse victims, was not the case and as such, I went on to never really return to a state of healthy equilibrium or balance until I chose to heal. There was either the state of numbed terror or full-blown terror, numbed fear or abject fear, numbed anxiety or anxiety. It became a mute button—the feeling was still there and running its ragged program but it was held at a distance. This created a chasm though, a deep, dark separation from myself and my reality.

I was stuck on this red alert for as long as I could remember. I wondered what even was a state of being without that as the guide? It seemed so important. It was what I believed would keep me safe. Even though logically, I eventually could see that it hadn't kept me safe very much as an adult, it felt practically impossible to let go of. I didn't consciously tell myself to dissociate, it just happened. I didn't know exactly what to say or do in certain circumstances, I just did them. It was super hard to come back into my body. And when I say come back, I don't know that I remember when I started leaving my body to survive. I didn't do it on purpose. I had no idea I was even doing it. I blocked so many things out. I developed this laser focus on what seemed necessary to not get me in trouble. I desperately needed to do everything right and always had this lurking feeling at the back of my mind that I was doing everything (well more like something) wrong. When the abuse was too much, I went away. I dissociated. It wasn't by conscious choice but by basic survival instincts. It makes sense though. Who would be able to be present for that amount of abuse?

The C-PTSD brain and memory. Childhood abuse and memory. I want to speak a little bit about this. It is like the brain is running there screaming its bloody head off on all these red alerts, and let me tell you, once you start listening to them, eventually fires just start to spring up everywhere. And if you let it, it just turns into one big out-of-control forest fire with seemingly no way out. There are billows of smoke, burning trees, buildings falling and it becomes harder and harder to breathe--there's no where safe to go, nothing left that's safe to do, nothing left that's safe to say or speak or eat or hear or say or do! It becomes this dark, constricting vice around you and it gets tighter and tighter and tighter. And eventually just when you need a bit of relief, it starts to relax...just a hair. And from this place of relief, it somehow finds a renewed state of vigor and begins at a whole other level of battering and rampage. And with these high levels of cortisol, that stress hormone, pumping out at full max speed all the time, it shuts off/represses functions like memory. Memory isn't really all that important if you might DIE. Whoa, die?

Sure, those times happen for everyone once in awhile but it can feel like that to a person with C-PTSD or someone who's been severely abused all the time. Something small can actually be seen (and felt in the body) as a life-ending possibility or the worst thing ever. And logically, one can look at it and see that is it an exaggeration, wayyyyy blown out of proportion but one just can't emotionally tap into that. Somewhere deep inside it resonates as true; this is indeed of the utmost importance and saving is necessary. So, a trauma survivor may struggle to remember what happened. And because they've been taught their whole lives to feel like they don't know and that they are overexaggerating, they can start to wonder if there is something wrong with them. Mentally remembering all the details isn't required for healing to occur. One may remember it all or only bits and pieces. One might have debilitating flashbacks or one might just have this fog. Our bodies always know the truth. If we lean into our bodies, they will tell us the story. It's up to us if we want to listen to what it has to say. We can choose to invalidate it because that's just a "disease" or "aches and pains" or we can choose to listen to our bodies' messages to us. Healing is always available to us and every needed resource is at our disposal. It is our choice whether we utilize them or not.

I just always accepted what they said. I didn't question it. If anything, I always questioned myself. It was understood that they knew and I didn't. Or perhaps better explained, I was learning and I would know, is what I eventually thought would happen. Yet as I grew older, it became apparent that that was not the case. It was never that I knew. I was allowed to make my own choices but I was pressured, coerced, manipulated, guilted and shamed after if it was a choice that was not approved of or would affect the family image. If I reflect on it though, my choice, was it really my choice or simply the choice I was conditioned to accept and choose, value and desire?

Chapter 12

Like Sharks Who've Smelled Blood

The next segment is a journal entry from early on in my healing journey.

~

I want to scream and shout and throw all the computers and screens right at the wall! You had no right to do that. You had no right to trick me into doing that. I had no idea that was what you were doing. I would never have done it if I had known but you knew that so that's why you didn't tell me. What is wrong with you?! Why would you do that to someone? How was that moral, ethical, just or okay? You knew it wasn't but you did it anyway. Why couldn't you have had some self-control? Why couldn't you have just made money some other way? I was not your toy nor your object to profit off of yet you used me just like that. Then you tossed me aside when I wouldn't perform anymore or wasn't the age you wanted. What good was I to you unless I was your little whore? I dressed up in that little slutty outfit. I climbed up onto that cute little bed. I turned just the way you told me to. I spread my legs just like you taught me to and I moved my hands just like you said. I smiled, laughed and looked all coy just like we'd practiced and I'd recited in my head. I can't say I didn't have fun. That wouldn't be true. Getting off was something I craved and you really approved.

I didn't understand quite why you wanted me to dress like this or do it like that but I liked the attention, the approval and of course, the release. I was good at the performance and I had even myself convinced that it was a lot of fun. I covered up the fact that I was confused, scared and ashamed with all these other half-truths. A half-naked cowgirl is pretty cute to some, I guess. A pretty much naked cowgirl is even better to others, I guess. A little suede vest, completely unbuttoned and breast buds showing. A cowgirl hat on my head must have been pretty charming. A little, pleated, jean mini skirt and some cowgirl boots topped off the cute little look. No undies, okay, I get it, I'll take them off too.

"Crawl up on the bed now, sit on your knees. Unbutton your vest for me, please. Slower, slower, there you go," you told me.

"Sorry, sorry, I didn't mean to do it wrong," I apologized.

"Let me see your little breasts. Ahh so cute. Lean forward and show me them, they are so cute. Touch them for me please, you know how to do it," you coaxed.

"I do!" I readily agreed, eager to please you.

"Okay, Cowgirl, now rise up on your knees and spread your knees apart along the bed so there's room for you to go for a ride on the bed. Pretend you're going on a horse back ride; you need room for the horsie," you said.

"Okay, sure, I know what to do," I replied, happy that I knew what to do.

"Now slip your hand between your legs and start to ride. Swing the lasso with your other hand. Good girl, you're doing it just right!" you praised.

I felt so happy inside that I was doing it right! I tried even harder.

"Drop the lasso and use both hands. Pull up your skirt and show me your pee-pee. Oooh ride your hips around, yum yum!" you told me.

I felt the cool breeze. I was a bit embarrassed but I tried so hard still.

"Now spread your pee-pee apart and do whatever to feel good. You've been such a good girl; show me how a good cowgirl feels good," you urged.

Yay, this wasn't so bad!

"Ride your hands. Get ready for the real ride soon," you instructed.

I just kept doing what he said without much thought. I didn't want to get it wrong and I felt like I didn't know what I was doing. I just kept trying harder though and he wasn't getting mad so I was encouraged by this.

"Oooooh you did such a good job! Look at your hands. They are soaking wet! Show me them, oooooh. Lick them," you told me.

That was kind of gross but okay, whatever I did what he wanted.

"Rub them over your nipples. Look at the dirty cowgirl!" you called out.

Dirty? I didn't want to be dirty. I guessed I was dirty. I should wash this off.

"Turn onto your hands and knees and show me your cow girl back side. Ooooh yeah, lift up your little skirt. Are you ready for the real ride?" you asked.

I started shaking because I was so excited. I worked really hard. I tried so hard to do it right, "Oh yes, Daddy, please!" I cried.

"No, you did it wrong! It's Cowboy! You messed it up!" he scolded as he smacked my bum. "Bad cowgirl!" Smack! Smack! Smack!

"I'm sorry, Daddy, I mean, Cowboy, I didn't mean to!" I said quickly. I was so mad at myself.

He kept smacking my bum as he pushed my face down in the bed. "Bad cowgirl, no ride for you!" he punished. He pushed me off the bed and told me to leave.

I saw his hard private, the one I had been performing for. I was so wet and ready for his hard private but I didn't say anything. I just walked out of the room and went down the hallway. I felt ashamed and a bit mad, a bit betrayed. I did it for the reward and now it was a no? I turned back and went back to the room. There was a small crack in the door that I could see through. I saw him standing there. Behind him was the bed on the right, a small lamp, and it was almost like a bunk bed. On the left was a desk with maybe some old computers or televisions. He beckoned to someone I couldn't see to the left of the door/me and then a bunch (3-5) of these orange people/ beings came running through. They ran to the bed and started removing all these cameras and recording devices that I hadn't seen. I was completely mortified. I felt like the floor was falling out beneath me. I couldn't breathe. I started to feel numb and cold and sweaty. I started to feel faint. I felt my face burning with shame, maybe anger, tears welling but not even coming up.

~

If I had remembered this earlier on in my healing journey, I would have absolutely lost my mind. I would have felt so utterly disgusted and mortified, so ashamed and embarrassed. I felt some of that as I remembered but I also felt so happy, relieved even, to have it out. I had that part shoved down inside of me for probably over 20 years. I was probably around 10 years old so yeah, more than 20 years. I carried that shame and that belief that I was a bad, dirty cowgirl who screwed it all up and now everyone knows, everyone can see it all too whenever they want. Never mind just that they could all see me naked and see me having so much fun playing with myself (I had really been into it, it was so much fun) on the recordings, now they could all know how I liked doing those dirty, bad things and that I did them wrong too! And they could see me get spanked too for doing such a bad job. It was all just so embarrassing. How could he not give me the hard reward? I only did it for the hard reward, I mean, I did it for the attention and to get off, but the incentive/reward was the cock and it was gone.

And then to find out that it was recorded; it was all staged and all our little games and fun were not our games and fun. He and she had got me to do it so they could record it. I didn't know anything about selling it at that age but what I did know was that now they could watch it whenever and everyone could know what bad things I did. They'd know that I was such a dirty, little whore who liked being daddy's good, little girl. You see, it took a long, long time for me to realize that that was not my shame to carry. It was not my fault that they manipulated and coerced a child. It was not my fault that they shamed and guilted a child. It was not my fault that I was groomed and conditioned that way. It was not my fault that they punished me and recorded it all. It was not my fault and it didn't make me a bad or dirty girl. And for the longest time, even though I could understand that in my mind, my heart still held on to that shame and that core belief that it was my fault and I was dirty, damaged and a bad girl. How did I let go of it? Persistance. I kept clinging to the truths I knew and even though those lies kept trying to slide their way back in, I kept searching for the truth, trusting that as I continued on this journey, that which was meant to stay would stay and that which needed to fall away would.

These two sides have waged war in my head. Screaming at me, demanding, taking…my choice taken away. I hated them sometimes for what they've taken away from me with their sick, perverted, psychological abuse. And their followers fell for it; they sucked it up like little piglets on the teat. Then I hated myself because I realized that they didn't take it—I gave it to them. It was coerced, manipulated and feared out of me but at the end of the day, I gave it to them. It's just so sickening, the way they take advantage of the victims...it's like they smell it like a shark smells blood. And they circle and they circle and you just don't even know that they're circling but you feel it. You feel them closing in around you but you feel helpless to do anything about it...until they open their mouths, their big, sharp shark mouths and they don't just go for the kill. No, they enjoy ripping you apart piece by piece. They watch the blood drip and grin there with the blood dripping out of their mouths. And just when you think you can't take anymore, they keep going but never enough to kill, because somehow you always wake back up in this nightmare, this torture that never stops.

And I don't know that I can ever truly explain to you how it all felt unless you've experienced it too. People have always looked at me and it's felt that either they've thought that I had it all together, that I was fine or they saw the pain and walked away. I felt that I had no other choice. I can't tell you the number of times I've faked that I was fine when I was hemorrhaging inside. Countless times I've helped others and given of myself even while the demons were screaming at me inside to just go away and die. I can't tell you how many sleepless nights turned into sleepy days that I still pushed through and got it done. And oh, how they would scream at me, berate me, shame me, knock me down further because I didn't get it all right, all done. I felt like I couldn't tell anyone. Speaking out meant getting in more trouble and I just didn't believe in myself enough to make that not happen. So, I just shut down. I made myself smaller and smaller until it seemed like there was nothing left. And yet, I still kept going because I didn't want to give up completely. To me, that would have signified that they had won and I just didn't want to let that kind of evil win.

All my life, I felt like people exploited me, used me…all while I was stupid, I mean naïve, enough to not even really see it. Or if I did see it, I just lied to myself that it wasn't that bad so I could attempt to survive. When I got married, I was naïve enough to believe that this relationship would just be better. That magical thinking got me a lot of pain. I turned a blind eye to the caustic truth in front of me and within me. I was so unwilling to look at the unhealed pieces of myself that I just stood there and took whatever abuse he hurled at me. Sure, I fought it sometimes but I would get so triggered and I was so utterly alone that I felt like I had no other choice. Those moments of what felt like complete and utter betrayal. The vile words hurled at me. The acts of abuse I accepted after I capitulated to his lies about my worth that only resonated with the vile truths I'd accepted from my childhood abusers.

His traumas intertwined with mine and we kept repeating these sick dance moves, over and over again. The psychological twisting of the truth to fit the story he wanted portrayed was directly proportional to the abuse he received as a child. And in the moments where I had complete clarity, I would watch us from a distance and see that generations of trauma were playing out right in front of me. And I would feel like I was in a sacred place bearing witness to something so very profound. Together, we consciously and unconsciously unearthed (and continue to unearth) generations of trauma and chose to do everything in our power to stop the cycle. As more and more of the sick evil and abuses done to us and stored within us were brought to the surface and released with as much emotion as when it was shoved there, I saw that we were in a spiritual war, I believe, for the collective conscious. Don't ever think that any moment is unimportant. Everything is of vital importance and yet it is insignificant. And it is in that balance that peace, clarity and surrender can flood in. As I started to rise and he chose to open himself, we found something we had never known before yet we intimately knew.

I remember looking forward to my grandparents putting me to bed when they came to visit. My parents didn't put me to bed so I guess, I felt cared for, loved, etc. by them doing so. They always spent a lot longer in my room than in my brothers' rooms though and I guess this made me feel special. I also just assumed it was because we would sing songs, in harmony, and it was something I liked. But I remember my grandmother shutting the door to my room and me getting all these feelings about it. I remember her bringing in her camera. I remember my pink and purple pajama set--I had two of the same ones and that had always been weird to me and I felt bad about that. They were special, expensive sets my mother had bought me from La Senza girls (the fancy girls lingerie store) --a button-up collared t-shirt and little shorts.

I remember my grandmother telling me to lie on the bed (now that I know the terms "doggie style") with those pajamas on and her taking pictures, praising me with "good girl". I remember her telling me to unbutton my shirt and her taking pictures. I remember her telling me to ride Creampuff with them on and her taking pictures. I remember her telling me to ride Creampuff with nothing on and her taking pictures. Always telling me "Good girl" after. No wonder I hated the term 'good girl'. I remember her telling me to take Creampuff away and open my legs and she took pictures after I was all excited. I remember her or maybe my grandfather touching my pee-pee with Creampuff. I remember them using their hands. I remember feeling bad about the gross stuff that was down there that was on their hands. I remember them telling me to straddle the foot board and ride along it. It was a square edge and it hurt but they didn't care and made me do it anyhow. I remember them pushing me backwards so I was lying on the bed with my knees over the footboard and it hurt the back of my legs from the sharp edges. I remember her leaning over with her camera.

I remember them making my legs go apart and them looking at my pee-pee. I would feel so embarrassed. And they wouldn't let me go and they would take pictures of it and me. They would hold me and they would touch me and I would feel so embarrassed. I couldn't get away and they would keep touching it. It felt so good and it was so embarrassing. I would "pee" myself and I would feel so embarrassed. I couldn't stop moving and I would feel the burning in my cheeks. And they wouldn't stop. I would be crying and they would keep going. It would burn in my pee-pee and I couldn't move to get away. And they would keep going even when they were hurting me and I wanted them to stop. They would use these loud machines that I thought everyone would hear. They would hold my legs apart and put it on my pee-pee. It would hurt and it would feel good. I wouldn't be able to stop myself from moving around and peeing and it would go on and on. And she would take pictures or videos and it was so gross and disgusting. I was embarrassed because I also liked some of it too and I wanted it to happen sometimes because it felt so good.

I used to hate having to write about this. It made me feel sick inside to think about this stuff, talk about this stuff, write about this stuff. I was hung up on not wanting it to be real. I wanted to pretend that it was all a big, sick joke. In the beginning, I would write, I would remember, and then I would be flattened by it all. I would have to stop, take a break and wait for weeks until I was able to stomach it again. It felt like I was being split back open, broken again from the inside out dragging all this shit up. This dirt, this blackness, this heavy rock, it felt like it ripped me open and cut me in a million different ways when I brought it up. It has been very relieving to remember though, to talk about it and get it out.

And it has also been incredibly painful and triggering. It has sent me into fits of dissociation. I've been overcome with immense amounts of shame and guilt. The panic has set in sometimes and basic tasks became extremely difficult. For example, I would recount the number of sandwiches I'd made for lunch 3 times and still wouldn't know if I'd made enough for everyone because I'd be in such a state of complete overwhelm. This shit is real. This shit is hard. This shit is a lot. And it has felt like an attack sometimes. It has felt like they've known when I'm getting into it, when I'm getting closer to exposing their dark truths. And I have felt like they do attack me or the safeguards they put in place to keep me quiet attack me. I've been hit with debilitating migraines, vomiting and stuck in bed crying from the pain for a few days at a time. Everything became immensely overwhelming and scary a few times too many.

To those who don't understand, I could see the perspective that I've been lazy, a bad housekeeper, a recluse, etc. I too had agreed with them sometimes and I heaped the blame and insults upon myself for not performing better at my basic tasks too. I've sometimes not given myself enough grace to deal with this stuff. I've said, well, I was a kid when it happened and I made it through all alone, I should be able to remember it without having any or only minimal reactions. But it's not that cut and dry. That pain was there. I shoved it down with pain and a lot of it has come up with pain. And some of it has been so fricking hard to let go of when it came up. Sometimes, I just wanted to hold on to it because somehow, I believed I could take that anger and hurt them with it. It was disgusting and I felt so infuriated that they did those things to me. They had no right and it felt like there was nothing I could do about it. They did it over and over again and I was stuck either pretending it didn't happen or living with the shame that I was the damaged goods they did it to. I've felt like I was marked as this disgusting being and everyone knew it to the point that my kids would walk all over me because I had such little self-respect without even knowing it.

I've had to look inward and be honest about some anger and resentment I held towards one of my kids because of it...I knew it wasn't his fault that he chose to treat me like dirt. On the one hand, I knew that it was my responsibility to enforce boundaries and demand that respect from him and on the other hand, the other kids grew up in the same environment and they didn't have that kind of meanness in them to be like that towards me. I could also see though that it wasn't his fault that he watched his father treat me with a lot of disrespect for a good part of our marriage with no consequence as it likely just looked like I allowed it to happen (because frankly, I did). And it was extremely painful to look at all the ways I had poured myself out and gave of myself to that kid for him just to turn around and spit in my face and say that I was a bad guy because I said no to him.

It was gutting to listen to them all side with my husband over skewed half-truths and one-sided misrepresentations because I had showed them that that was all I was worth. I would do something a few times and they'd say that didn't count and my husband would help make supper one time and then they'd say he helps make suppers. It was like listening to my parents and brothers all over again minus the physical raping. And while I was sick of being the scapegoat for everything, I also didn't know how to change it. I didn't care enough, I guess, to fight about these things or demand differently. Maybe I didn't feel like I deserved any better or differently. And they had such brilliant arguments for why I shouldn't be treated any differently. They made sense and they didn't make sense. I'd be trapped over and over again in this haze of pain and confusion and terror and I was left feeling so apathetic wondering if it would ever end.

Chapter 13

Good Girl

I've also really struggled with letting go of the shame. There was this voice that kept whispering, no, screaming, that it was all my fault, I've screwed everything up, everyone will hate me and so on. I've let go of that voice, a lot. But still, it creeps in sometimes. I feel it in the clenching of my jaw, the migraines, the grinding of my teeth, the rigidness, the fear and lack of joy that sometimes is there. And I can hear her telling me it's all my fault. That voice of my mother, even just that look on her face. The way she would tsk tsk and I would jump in line. She'd argue she never did that and maybe she didn't do it on purpose. Maybe it was sometimes a subconscious thing she did, perhaps something that has been passed down through the generations. And I wonder if I do that with my kids too?

That very thing that scarred me so much, I wonder if I, in my fear of doing it all wrong, of getting in trouble, of ruining everything, if I've unconsciously caused them to pick up those feelings from me? I don't want it to be that way but I've run on unconscious programming for a long time and it would be remiss of me not to consider that possibility. And I'm sorry that my lack of emotional knowledge, my lack of teaching them these things because I didn't know them, the trauma and it's symptoms that ran me for so long has impacted them. I am so grateful for this healing journey and I'm glad it's not twenty years from now but I am still sad that I didn't heal sooner. I am sorry that I probably hurt them through my fears and anxieties, this cloud of shame, the way I've bled out on everyone. And I wish I could just completely rip it off, just be done with this pain and be completely healed. But maybe that's where they want us, blaming and beating ourselves up, wishing to change a past we cannot change. And so, in accepting I find so much grace and freedom to be.

I met someone recently. I think she could have been me, I mean a me I would have been if I hadn't left, if I hadn't escaped their clutches. I'll bet if you were to ask her, she'll defend them and say that her family was just trying to help. She'll say that she was the one who was wrong and the one who put them out. She'll say that she's the one who wasted their time and dragged them around on a childish whim.

She'll admit fault and accept the blame that she should've known better--they have the experience and who is she to question them? I had to meet her/her family more than 3 times for me to sort of even see it. I'm not even sure yet that I see it all. Clueless. Innocent. Naïve. Head up her ass or up in the clouds...or maybe, head buried in the sand. Living a fantasy. Behind a façade. Lost in her role. Too close to it. Low self-esteem. Scared. Unsure of herself. Dependent. Beaten down. Abused but high-functioning so only those who know know. So, I write to speak out for the little girls like me, the women who I could've been. You're not alone and the role they carved out for you? You don't have to fulfill it. It's okay to resign and live the life you want.

I want to talk about how it felt to be at their mercy. Helpless. Just a pawn for them, a toy. I walked around clueless, truly feeling like it was all my fault. My mother would talk me up--that I was this great baker and then get me to bake something completely new and difficult, a homemade from scratch blueberry pie made from frozen berries. Anyone who knows anything about cooking fruit pies, especially from frozen berries, knows how difficult it is to prevent them from being runny. I didn't and I made this pie for her special guests, the pastor and his wife from church. And she told me how the pie was so runny. It tasted good but ran all over their plates. On and on she went to the point that I never made blueberry pie again. I felt so embarrassed because I had let her down. I felt like I was a bad baker, a bad person and a bad guy for ruining this. I was probably 14. I wonder if she was even talking about the actual blueberry pie.

It was always so confusing. There were so many rules and on the one hand, I loved the rules because rules can be followed and on the other hand, these weren't normal rules. These rules, they could change or reinterpret them at will. Which, I guess, is pretty "normal" (it's normal because it's all around us but please don't confuse normal with right) if you look around at the world we live in. Take the Canadian government, for example. There's a long list of crimes they've committed (according to their own rules), yet they go virtually unpunished. It didn't matter how hard I tried, some days, I always got it wrong. It was so confusing because deep down I knew I had gotten it all right, followed all the rules and yet, there I was with her sitting on my face again or shoving me in the closet and unzipping her jeans. It was always my fault that she was doing this to me. If only I hadn't embarrassed her in front of her friends, the pastor no less!

But this deep-seated feeling of always being wrong, of getting it wrong, of it being my fault, of being in trouble was always there and has been extremely hard to release. It can't be rationalized. It hadn't been my fault. I hadn't done something actually wrong or even if I did, no child deserves to be abused as punishment. There was no way I deserved the glue stick on my genitals while tied to the chair or being strung up in the closet upside down, left alone in the dark. Yet, I was so demoralized and so desperately dependent on them being a child that I believed that I did. Why else would this be happening? I want you to see how confusing it all was and how there was no one there to help me make sense of it. Everyone just said (or showed me) that it was my fault. In my head, if it was my fault, I could somehow justify their actions. I could live with it, at least kind of, that they were doing these things to me because I had screwed up. If I had missed spraying the spot on the hard wood floor or worse, I had sprayed the spot and then forgotten to go back and wipe it a few minutes later so now the spray had been sitting in a puddle on the wood floor and I'd probably ruined it— this justified their actions in my mind, at least to some extent.

It was a systematic break-down of me psychologically. I knew that I hadn't broken the necklace but it was her word against mine and no one ever believed me versus her anyway. I hadn't painted the chip on the head board of my bed but she insisted I had done it for who else could have done it. But even though I knew deep down that I hadn't done it, I was so accustomed to believing there was something wrong with me, accepting that everything was my fault as well as feeling ashamed and guilty, that a part of me always resonated with their reasoning and I would accept or maybe better to say, I would submit. Frankly, it was just easier to accept their whatever rather than fight it. They always won anyhow and it was just easier to get it over with and less painful/less severe if I just submitted. It was so important for them always to win and I just didn't care enough or just realized that I never really could win anyhow. It was beyond confusing, disheartening and apathy inducing to be one day encouraged by them to do something and then to so radically be punished for it the next.

I remember going downstairs into the basement at my parent's home when I was around 15 years old to discuss with my parents how I needed their support. The medical professionals on the eating disorder ward had said that I needed family support and encouraged me to ask for it. My parents had said there that they would be there for me and I believed them. But a few months into my recovery, I found that they really weren't supportive at all and I called them out on it--begging, sobbing for their support, explaining how alone I felt and how it felt like they didn't care, on and on. Of course, they said they were sorry and that they would try harder. They said they just didn't want to make it worse but they would try to improve. So, as the relief and warmth started to flood in, I then found that I was up on the pool table and my brother was there too.

I was naked on the table and I was splayed completely open, sitting on the one end of the table. And they shot pool balls at my vagina and vulva. It hurt and no one cared. I had to sit like that. I just had to sit there and let them do whatever they wanted. Internally, I was beating myself up for being so stupid to have believed them that they wanted to help me. I berated myself for being so selfish to have asked for help. And in the midst of my self-hating, I found myself on my back. My head was hanging off the pool table and they were shoving the pool cues in my vagina and butt. My parents took turns putting their parts in my face--my father's penis down my throat, my mother's vulva at my mouth. And I don't know if I could have fought it or if I was drugged or too afraid or felt too ashamed or was just so trained that my job was to submit.

And that was it. My job was to submit. My role was to go do anything on the acceptable list of activities (baking, crafts, reading, schoolwork, play outside, chores) and await their desires. And their desires, whatever they were, were mine to fulfill. That was the attention they gave me. I realized it wasn't dogs that I hated but that my parents treated their dogs with more regard than me. And I say regard because my basic needs were met but nothing more. I was a very self-sufficient child and I think I would have been okay if they would have just ignored me completely and left me alone. Later on, I'm sure looking back I would have seen that I was neglected but ultimately it wouldn't have mattered much because I was fulfilled by the ways I gave myself self-care. I was a very resilient child and didn't need much. I preferred being alone. I didn't feel neglected if no one talked to me or helped me do this or that. I was fiercely independent and quite introspective. What left the deep, deep marks on me though was the psychological and sexual abuse. If the abuse had just been purely sexual, I think I then too would have been hardly traumatized. I would have been able to look back and say wow, they were some pretty messed up, traumatized people and I'm sorry they grew up in such circumstances that they felt they should treat their own daughter that way. It was that twisted, dark, psychological torture that ate at my soul.

It was the sudden sheet lifted in the night and the dick up my ass. It was the hands around my throat so I couldn't breathe or scream all while they screamed it was my fault and told me what a disgusting little whore I was. It was the flashing of the camera knowing they were recording the disgusting and shameful things they were doing. It was the blood on the floor, my blood, that they made me clean up because it was my fault I'd made such a mess. It was the hypocrisy that it was okay for them to touch me or make me touch me but it was not okay for me to do so unless commanded. It was the confusion that this was okay to do and yet we couldn't tell anyone. It was the horror when I truly realized how much of a slut they had trained me to be and how they had recorded a lot of it. It was the humiliation and feeling of being ruined when I realized that now everyone could know and watch/see that disgusting stuff. It was the disgust with myself for longing for it, craving sex and an orgasm all the time.

You see, it was my fault that my father was friends with my brother and not me because I didn't like movies and he did. It didn't matter the true reasons that I didn't want to watch movies alone with him in the basement. It was always my fault. I'd caused it to be this way. I loved the rules because they were like a test I could ace…except this test often had a faulty answer key and I could never predict when that would be. Sometimes I'd get it wrong even though I knew I'd gotten it right. And sometimes I'd get it all right but then they'd still be mad or violent or even just do it and I couldn't rationalize why. It must have been because of me, because I'd done something wrong. When I hit puberty and got my periods, I would sometimes not shower for long periods of time and let my hair get super greasy so that I would look bad. I wouldn't change my pads until they were extremely full and gross. I'd leave my pads stored in a drawer in my room, all used. I guess these were just ways to get back at them, to try to make myself gross and disgusting but they still came anyway. Dirty girls have to do dirty things.

I remember getting picked up by my grandparents on one of those days to go record for their CDs and feeling bad that I hadn't showered but also not caring because I didn't really want to go there anyway. I mean, I kind of did, but I kind of didn't. The singing and recording of the singing was fine; it was just that part where it turned into something else that I didn't really like. Their producer was a slimy, old guy and I didn't really like him except I kind of did because sometimes it felt good and I knew deep down that I was being helpful, I guess. I mean, it was a part of the job. And I would feel bad accepting the money or the royalties and also feel like I deserved it too, for the work I'd done. I don't know how to really explain to you the helpless terror I lived through over and over. And how I lied to myself that it wasn't terror and that I was okay. It was justified as the fear of God or a healthy fear of sin/death. These are justified as ways to get you to repent. And all the ways they get you to repent. And then they get to stand there and say haha, nothing happened. She's making it up. She doesn't even know what she's talking about. See, she's crying, she's just scared of a spider, she's a really emotional child, she doesn't know what's going on, we are getting her all the help she needs.

She will say she helped me by taking me out of public school when I was screaming/sobbing every day and homeschooling me. And on the one hand, I will agree that

homeschooling was a beautiful choice for me. But emotionally, no one ever helped me deal with what it was that caused that kind of reaction. No one helped me identify it. The principal just walked me around the halls all alone until I calmed enough. They just took me out of school or kept me home before the year ended and that was that. Problem solved. And I don't disagree; I was much happier. But that trauma was never looked at. You don't go from happy to go to school to screaming your bloody head off sobbing in terror at seven years of age at the flick of a switch for no reason.

But no one asked those questions or if they did, no one helped me figure it out. I remember watching my grandparents' motorhome turn down the off ramp and go onto the highway as we kept going to school. They were leaving after visiting us and I remember thinking/hearing in my head that I was never going to see my grandfather (my safest person) again. And then something happened and I couldn't handle going to school. I started screaming and sobbing--the teacher would have to pull me from my mother. The principal would have to walk me around the halls to avoid a scene at the classroom. But no counseling was done, nothing. And I wonder why all those adults didn't do anything else and if their thoughts were that I was just a spoiled kid having a fit.

I remember my mother coming to visit me when my oldest was a newborn. She had brought me some shorts to wear for boating as we were going on a trip and I had said I might need something to wear. She also brought me a tea--I remember the red cup from the coffee shop with the apple cinnamon tea and the two sugars. I remember setting it on the change table in our room. I remember going with her into my husband and I's bedroom and trying the shorts on in front of her. I remember her looking at me and telling me how good I looked. She said no one would know that I had just had a baby. I don't remember where my son was but I remember her and I were then on our bed rolling around, tangled up in each other's arms. And I was energetically going through these motions without thinking, without feeling. It was just like I was acting out a play with a script that someone had given me.

Then it was over, just like always, and she was leaving. It had felt like she had just gotten there and she said she'd been there a long time (and by the time, she had) but somehow the time just had slipped by. I'd wondered at the time how it was so--we had only just played with the baby and had lunch. How had it taken so long? When I remembered later, then I knew. I just pretended that everything was okay though. I lied to myself that I didn't feel hollow inside and sick. I just was so used to doing whatever she wanted that I didn't even really think about it anymore. I didn't feel I had any choice. There was no other way. I just slipped into this kind of auto-pilot and that was that. Maybe she drugged me, maybe she hypnotized me, maybe she used some frequency, maybe she triggered me or maybe I was just so programmed, so demoralized that I just did it without thinking, like a good little girl.

Chapter 14

True Power Within

I think because my family checked off most boxes for people, no one really thought twice about me. We were a well-off, white, Christian family. People just labelled me as a perfectionist, an over-achiever, a type A, goodie-two shoes, super Christian, etc. And perhaps because those types are desired, no one really questioned it. It was my fault that I was like that and I was choosing to be like that, were only a few of the excuses they used. I was the one putting so much pressure on myself. It is good that she's so devoted to God and her family. She puts such immense pressure on herself to do well--that's why she has migraines and cries. She's got an eating disorder because she tries too hard. She will make a great doctor as she's so smart, caring and devoted to her family and Church. Meanwhile, the dark truth was that I needed to be perfect or the results were extreme punishments. Even normal mistakes or accidents resulted in abuse so in an attempt to cope, I just tried harder and harder to do it all right. Like almost every child, I blamed myself for my parent's shortcomings and for the abuse they put on me. It was easier to accept that I was the problem rather than accept that my parents and family were actually committing these atrocious crimes against me.

I have felt like a loser. I can't disagree with that. There have been many times I have just accepted the words being screamed at me, the insults being hurled, the blame being dished out, the abusive force being asserted. I have cowered under their force. It has seemed true. I have believed it even when a part of me inside was screaming, 'NO!'". But I gave up so many times. I tried to speak out, tried to make people believe me but until my husband, no one has ever really cared that they did what they did. There were faces of shock, some empathy, some pity, some looks of horror. But ultimately, they just didn't seem to care because I look around me and where are they now? I've cried these tears alone. I've wiped up the blood alone. I've screamed in terror alone. I've sat shaking in the dark at night alone. And over and over, I've felt the sting of the blame, that it was my fault. It was always my fault if it happened and it was my fault when it happened again.

You're right, I did almost completely give up at one point. The police officer, the church people, the people at the sexual assault center, the psychologist, the psychiatrist, the doctors, the teachers, the seemingly friendly neighbor all did it too and eventually, the world just started to look like this terrible dark and scary place where no one could be trusted. And they all just looked at me like I was the crazy one…no one has ever believed the sobbing little ol' me. It was always the same old story—they knew what happened, I didn't. There were times I just accepted the abuse because I did feel ashamed and I did have guilt. It was not the guilt you might think I'm talking about. I mean, I was conditioned and programmed to feel guilty for making a normal kid mistake. Accidentally spilling the milk or forgetting to take out the trash--these little things were blown out of proportion as to be these huge sins and transgressions I had committed and for them I was taught to feel such immense guilt and shame. How could someone so smart act this way? I was conditioned then to accept and even need punishment to help ease this guilt, to sort of "forgive" these sins.

A spanking, a slap, a screaming at, rape, so on and so forth, abuses mislabeled as "punishment". It was so conditioned in me, so trained in me that I just checked out to manage the pain, to forget about the incidents, to somehow get through. I'd remember glimpses of it and shove the rest down, put it away in a tight little package in the far back corner of the drawer designated for the dark crap in my mind and lock it up with that special key. One day though, I found the key. Turns out I had it the whole time. The power was within me to remember and to forget. Knowing that gave me such peace and freed me from so much pain that was holding me down.

I do believe my experiences. I do believe in holistic healing. I do believe in trauma recovery. I do believe in herbal remedies. I do believe in natural childbirth. I do believe in protecting children. I do believe in every being's right to live on earth and take up space. I do believe that the earth is highly underpopulated in comparison to her size and that it is simply a "mismanagement" or intentional misuse of her resources that is the reason for most poverty, homelessness, starvation or disease. And I do want my voice to be heard. I have struggled at times to believe it is worth it and wondered if anyone cares to hear what I have to say. I have felt that those who may care already know and those who don't care won't care about what I have to say anyway. I have felt like I'm facing this giant. And I have wondered if the story of David and Goliath is even real.

It took a lot of soul-searching, a lot of feeling the pain and dwelling in the past before I realized that anymore was wasting my energy and getting sucked into the vortex of this mental prison. Where is this prison? Where are these emotions? Where is the harm? Where is the pain? Where is the fear? PRODUCE IT!! By carrying all this, I wondered if perhaps I was wasting my time, my being, squandering my purpose away? Then I wondered, what exactly is my purpose? Why does my purpose need to be any grander than any other of the creatures on this planet—be born, grow up, reproduce, care for offspring, die? Why do I need to do something meaningful, more meaningful than that? Then I looked at it and I thought to myself, how will I feel if I'm old and I see my children being abused and oppressed and I did nothing about it? If my daughters only have the likes of the evil midwife who I had (or her protégés) as midwifery options, will I be wishing I'd done something about it?

What if my daughter is forced into a c-section because of the mis-guided and biased medical professionals? What if my sons are unable to make money because they don't have the degree or medical status that is so deemed necessary then by the powers that be? What if we can't walk freely on the street because all our rights have been stripped completely away? What if there are kids who could have been helped because I spoke out about the sick abuse I endured and instead, they suffered in part because of my silence? I cannot control what others do. Looking back on my life though later on, I really can't think of a reason I would be upset that I had tried to effect change. And so, I keep coming back here to write. In the beginning, it was hard for me to trust and believe in myself. It took a lot of tries before I stopped the doubting, the shaming, the blaming and the not feeling good enough.

I'd have these moments of clarity and it all was put into perspective. It then suddenly didn't hurt or bother me as much and I felt okay. And then it would hit me like a loud sound in the night and I'd be stuck rocking back and forth in the fetal position begging for some sort of relief. And I mean that both figuratively and literally. There were times where it has been literally but mostly it was this figurative comforting of myself from the wild pain and fear that threatened to overtake me. I'm so sorry, I'm so sorry, I'm so sorry, I'm so sorry. I can't tell you the number of times I've scream-sobbed that one. Or I don't know what to do, I don't know what to do, I don't know what to do. And so, I went through life fixating on small things that I could control...my grades, volunteering, eating, exercising, cleaning fits, keeping myself busy with meaningless tasks, etc. etc. Trying to keep this pain under control, trying to self-regulate or soothe myself so I could continue to "function".

It wasn't until I truly rejected the lies they had burned into me about who I am that I was able to say, "No".

I had to look that shame right in the face and tell it that it didn't define me anymore. I had to choose to walk away from toxicity and step into the reality I wanted to create. When I let go of being a victim, I was able to acknowledge my part. Turns out, I'm pretty powerful and my words actually do mean something. Shockingly enough, when I demand respect, it happens. When I chose to rise up, there was nothing that could stop me because I believed it was something that would happen. When I realized that I didn't have to hold on to the pain of the abuse but that I could hold on to that beautiful, little girl inside me instead, I was able to unearth and transmute so many traumas I had buried inside. And all those outward abuses I was experiencing in my adult life, they fell away. They were simply mirrors to my inner pain and when I looked those in the face, unafraid, true healing came.

I believe that each and every one of us has the power to heal. We have been trained to give our authority away to all of these different systems in so far as to be a society that is so disconnected from themselves that most people are walking around traumatized and unconsciously perpetuating generational cycles of abuse. Our society has been structured now in such a way that most are barely surviving never mind thriving. I know I was. And as long as we are seeking outside ourselves for healing and guidance, I believe it will be even more challenging for true transformation to take place. That inner spark inside—that one they tried to get you to give up or extinguish? It may very well be the single most powerful thing you can ever get in touch with. Tap into that and I believe you can find meaning, unconditional love and true transmutation beyond what any words can express.

We will meet many teachers along our way but it is up to us to choose how we implement the lessons set before us. True power emerges when we are willing to release our grip on control, fear and the pain and instead, surrender to that which is both unknown and completely known. Our unconscious reaction to abuse and trauma may have imprisoned us but our conscious response can be the key that sets us free. Allow yourself to feel. Allow yourself to grieve. Allow the rage to burn. Allow whatever needs to bubble up out. Just don't stay there ruminating in the pains of the past. Forgiveness and forgetting don't have to go hand in hand. Trust that you do know, that you are worthy of taking up space and ultimately, that you are, you were and you always will be.

About the Author

Erika Burton graduated with a Bachelor of Social Work degree from Dalhousie University. A survivor of childhood sexual and psychological abuse, she spends her time writing and counseling others who want to holistically heal trauma. She is an advocate for holistic healing, both on a personal and global level. She is a homeschooling and homesteading mother to a large crew of kiddos and speaks as well about the journey of healing while parenting. What once almost killed her, now she works to help those who have similar struggles. From an eating disorder to self-harm to debilitating nightmares and panic attacks, the author writes from a place of authenticity, spreading hope and holistic healing. Her mission--to expose the dark truths about abuse and join others in awakening true holistic healing and wellness in all. She has an online presence at HALV ROUNDTABLE Holistics.

www.ingramcontent.com/pod-product-compliance
Lightning Source LLC
Chambersburg PA
CBHW021144130626
46554CB00005B/1654